# INTRODUCTION.

I wrote this book called **A Pencil in God's Hand in the life of a child**. In this book there is no talk or reference to any religion based it is about the fact that we are all controlled by a higher power in order to do good in a life of a child, whether he comes from a broken family, or a healthy family. There was a saying " it takes a village to raise a child" and that means that everyone in the community takes part in raising the child every action the next person takes and does affect a child in the community, from saying please and thank you or to being helpful to the fellow neighbor.

In this book you will read about life space work. Now life space work is working in the moment where the child is at. Whether it is in the playground, bedroom, yard, park, or wherever he sleeps when you do life space work it means that any moment is use as a learning moment. We will talk about routines and indigenous games, and working in the moment

The book is based on my personal experience in working in a children home with children coming from broken home and broken families, where they went through trauma that no child should ever face in their lives. In the book there is ways to deal with them and activities to do with, the difficult days and the good days and tips on what to do at certain moments.

# CHALLENGES CHILDREN FACE DAILY

Children today face many challenges in today's society. I was also faced with many challenges and it saddens me to think that today's youth will face the same challenges as I did. I fell victim to the influences of negativity, but I opened my eyes and made a change for the better. By examining the root causes, we can identify solutions to help today's youth avoid making uninformed decisions.

## Poverty- We All Affected By This

**Unemployment:** Parents are unemployed because there are not enough jobs. As a result, they will do whatever it takes to put clothes on their children's backs and food on the table.

**School Drop-Out:** Many children living in poverty will drop-out of school because they are bullied, or they don't feel that they fit in. They may also be ashamed because their families are unable to afford school fees such as lunch money, field trip fees etc.

**Uneducated Parents:** A shocking number of parents are have only attained low levels of education. This low level of education becomes generational as parents struggle to assist their children with school work. Uneducated parents are also unable to understand the school curriculum.

**Low Self Esteem:** Children in poverty also suffer from low self-esteem. They do not believe in themselves because they have been bullied or pressured into making poor decisions. Youth are becoming prey to adults who they believe will support them, such as "Sugar Daddies", "Blessers", or "gangster" boyfriends. Young women are becoming pregnant by men who cannot help them support their children. As a result, these young women are forced to rely on government aid. Boys are influenced by clothes(name brands) and bullied into becoming gangsters or end up drug abusers. Have unrealistic goals and live life passing by, day by day

**Parent and Child Communication**: Children and teens do not feel confident enough to speak to their parents about sensitive topics and their true feelings. In addition, parents are ill-equipped to be active listeners and offer positive advice to their children.

# Effects

Because of the poor conditions that poverty creates children between the ages of twelve and eighteen are being bullied, joining gangs, using drugs, and becoming victims of sexual and domestic violence. Teens are using drugs as a way of escape, or to hide their disappointments. Teens are also running away from home and becoming involved with abusive men. They are becoming pregnant at an early age or being raped by abusive men. To exacerbate the problem, young women will stay in an abusive relationship because they are unable to support themselves. They do not have any employable skills or proper education.

# THE PENCIL IN GOD'S HANDS
## in a life of a child

## What is a pencil?

*Q. What does it do? What is their purpose? Why were they designed this way?*

> *A.  A pencil is used to write and draw. Rough sketches are drawn with a pencil before finishing touches are applied and final copies are issued. Great masterpieces started with the first sketches being drawn with a pencil. We can see that a pencil is used to make a mark. We can be like God's pencil in the lives of children.*

*Q.  So, how are we going to make a mark in the lives of children? Will my mark be positive? How will I be a leader who guides children to success and motivates, uplifts, supports them? How will I guide them to achieve their goals and make them the leaders of tomorrow.*

> *A.  I want you to remember, to do this you must be the adult. You will need to have a positive attitude, and be spontaneous and flexible. You will need to be consistent and able to effectively communicate. Most importantly, you must respond rather than simply reacting.*

# A Pencil Uses Lead

Lead is what the pencil uses to make it's mark. Without the lead a pencil is useless. The lead within the pencil is what gives it its purpose. Just as the lead in the pencil, we must have an internal motivation or goal. My purpose as God's pencil, is to be a leader and role model in the lives of children. You must have your own purpose to be an effective tool.

Self Check
- Do I really want to be a leader in the lives of children?
- Why do I desire to make a difference in the development of children's identities?
- Do I know where I come from? How can my past experiences help me become a better leader?
- Do I know where I want to go? What kind of influence do I wish to have?

# A Pencil Needs a Hand for Assistance in Making a Mark

We all need support. My support is the team that I associate with. If we surround ourselves with positive people our outlook and attitude will be positive. My team gives me constructive criticism. When we are given constructive criticism we will be able to see that can always grow and improve.
being part of a part of a team is having the confidence to go to someone and ask for assistance there will be times when u feel u have had more than enough to deal with and in a team you  have someone to ask for assistance and guidance.

.

# Support

When I worked at the  children's home we had
an incident this one night when the  boys from
the  boys section decided that that they wanted
to do what they wanted and not go sleep, it was
just one of those days when everything that u
say the kids (boys) tend to challenge it. I have
been struggling with getting them to be calm
and into bed. Seeing that I was working alone in
the boys section my partner (Ms Angel ) she was
off sick that day and will be in the day after. So
there I was with 25 boys alone that felt that bed
times will be when they feel, now some kids
wanted to sleep but the older few wanted to
make noise throw shoes and be disruptive  Be
with the others. I was at my wits end and felt
like screaming with them going on.because we
have a dormItory system it was difficult to
separate them from each other, throwing them
out would only cause me more problems and
they would probably go on teasing the girls and
make noise that side. And what was more
frustrating is that I must still wake up very early
to make breakfast the next morning. so my team
(colleagues from the girl section) came over and
assisted me with the boys. one said (Tania) that I
can go over to the girl section where the kitchen
is  and take a break have a coffee then come over
(i need it cos I felt like I have reach boiling point)

so I went and had my cup of coffee and a
sandwich came back and the boys came up to
me and apologies and all got in their beds and
went to go sleep. I thank my colleagues (Tania
and Jody). The following day I had no problems
with the children and they were all respectful
and the older boys assisted me with the younger
boys

The boys saw that my team was supporting me
and as a team and that we were united in getting
them to bed. they did not bribe them or anything
they stood as firm, even though I was away for a
few minutes they got the message that they can
not  manipulate them and do as they please.
if my team did  not come and supported me I
would have probably lost it and be more
stressed and probably be overworked and
wouldn't be effective in working with the youth
that weekend. but thanks for the support of my
team.

When a new child is being admitted to our centre  into our centre we have a panel meeting that consist of Child and youth care worker (Me) the child (new) social worker (Lelani - residential social worker) Senior child and youth care worker/ supervisor (Claire) then parents (if they are available) external social worker and we have a meeting to discusses if our centre is a suitable place for the child, everyone has their input and say and then I take the child to see the centre and I explain to him what happens where and how and our routine rooster and duty rooster. this give me time to build some sort of connection with the child and talk to him when his guard is down(not suspicious) and in that time the other team members get to discuss information that cannot be discussed in front of the child, such as Behaviours at home, child drug abuse history, or any any kind of information that is to sensitive for the child to hear about, sometimes parents are to afraid to speak in front of the children. Depending on age of children and reason that they were taken away from the parents care.

When the tour is done we all get together and greet and say our goodbyes. I get informed what was discussed while I was with the child and vica versa then we sit and discussed if we are suitable to have the child in our centre. we make at that moment a decision as a team and we inform the external social worker of  our decision.

IF we choose that we are the correct centre for the child we will inform the external social worker and schedule a date for the child to come. We get a school transfer and look for a school for the child. Any medicine and hospital card for the child.
I go get toiletries for the new child  and clean bedding for the his bed have a meeting with my group of boys and inform them of our new child that is joining us.

# Crisistism

when I talk about criticisms in a team it must
constructive and not taken into another way,
criticism help you grow if you take it as
constructive.

I once handled a situation very unprofessionally
(lets say I lost my cool) and my colleagues came
and assisted me and we dealt with the situation
together. later the same day when all children
were settled and calm they called me aside and
we discussed how I dealt with the situation and
what way I was wrong and everything I did was
wrong (they could have reported me to the office
cause I sweared at a child who swore at me) but
they told me and criticised me on how I behaved
and I took it bad and felt hurt and bad but later
on I realised that they are just trying to help me
and guide me to become a better worker (Child
and youth care worker). I was still new to the job
but I took their advice and learned from it to
better myself and a person and as a worker in
the field of child care.

**Learning from team members**

We at Heatherdale children's home worked as sleep-in child care workers and we had a shift roster  where we come on duty at 13:30 on a monday and work till 08:30 on a wednesday morning we do get our off  time but when we on duty we sleep in. now on some of my off days I use to stay in at work and I watch how the other staff (team) works with the children and how they handle situation. Also I monitor the children's behaviour when the other team is on duty. That way I learned how to handle some children's behavior (Swearing, fighting, bullying) and how to behave when certain behaviour or situation arises and then I can improve myself and become a better child and youth care worker

# Standing united as a team

This one particular day we at the centre had a incident with a group of boys (names  are changed due to confidentiality)

addie - 11 years old  *He was a group leader, fast runner, love to do somersaults and backflips and can climb just about any building with just using his bare hands- father and other  adults used him to break into people's houses by climbing up the gutter pipes and open windows and do  house breakings and mischief that why they ended up in a child and youth care centre . he is very manipulative and when confronted by adults he uses his tears and manipulation to get out of trouble. Mom and Dad seperated we do not know the whereabout of the father, but mom stays in Langebaan, Western Cape, South Africa*

Waanie - 9  *years old he is addie brother small young and sweetest boy u will ever meet, loves his parents and he is just at the* centre to better himself and just a follow of his brother, cries easily and show remorse if he is in the wrong

John - 10 years old mother is a single mother has a history of drug abuse, john has experimented with weed (dagga) smoke cigarettes, and he has a tendency to steal, file showed that his father is in and out of jail for house breaking, robbing and stealing. john was caught for shoplifting and a further investigation showed that mom used him to do shoplifting and stealing from family and at shops,
he was a climber just as addie can easily climb a gutter piper to get to a window or a roof. he has two sisters at the centre younger than him
Saffie - 11 years old loves soccer raised by a single parent and has two other sibling younger than him at the centre, he is easily influenced and has a very bad temper when he gets angry, reason being in the centre is sisters was sexually molested by mom's boyfriend and mom still lives by him (case was still under investigation) and he refuse to go to school
Jack  - 11 years old Adhd diagnosed, easily influenced by others,  he is in the centre because of the abuse by grandmother, mother passed away and father is unknown, rest of family is from durban and contact with them is mostly telephonic or a visit if aunts come to cape town during Christmas. He has a very bad temper and has no impulse control because of the  ADHD diagnosis

Leam - 10 years old  he is his mother's golden goose (mother used him to gain financially for her drug habit, he is a very sweet good looking boy that can easily manipulate you and he loves to tell lies, currently he is under the care of foster parents which he loves going to every weekend but mother's was busy breaking that bond with the foster parents so that relationship (the mother told the foster parents that if they want to see the child they must pay her and look after her also, so foster parents decided not to do this anymore and just look after leam but mom took him out for the day with permission from social workers (our internal and external) and when he returned then he had an attitude and didn't want to go to foster parents)

at 13H00  on a monday afternoon  this group of boys decided to walk of our premises of the centre and made a stop at vangate mall which is a 15 min drive depending on traffic and it took them 40 minutes to walk to the mall and then they decided to do  some shoplifting at the Pick and Pay shopping mall and from there on addie (group leader) decided that they should walk to Langebaan (a 26 hour walk but they hike) and go to their mother and go their.

We at the centre when we realised the boys
where gone we gave them some times to come
back because whoever runs away they normally
just in the road outside and then they come back.
I did inform the Senior child and youth care
worker, Social worker, and the Director of the
centre and the Child and youth care workers on
duty. By 16H00 I took a walk down the avenues
with a group of senior boys from the centre and
Yvonne (Girls section child and youth care
worker) and we walk to the shops and the
corners and parks where they would normally
hang out. I came back informed the team that
they are nowhere to be found.
I was told by the seniors that I should give them
till 17h00  and phone the police and report the
case. at 17h05 I report the case to the police
(athlone police) and the said they will send a van
(police van)

Around 19H00 a car is sounding its horn at the gates I called to let the gate be open and a lady pulled up rude and very angry scolding that we are not a good centre and we cannot look after kids she will report us the the Department of Social Development. and out jump the boys warmly dress with new tops and each one with a party packet (packet with sweets, lollypops, chips and chocolate)  in their hands with the most saddest faces I ever have seen (manipulation) she was asking who is mr mo (Me) I told her that it is me and then she accused me of hitting the boys, kicking and swearing at them and if they are going to be left here I will let the bigger boys hit them. I was shocked when I heard the accusations, the lady gave me her card and told me that she refuse to leave the boys here and she will take them with her and bring them back when the director and social worker are here. I looked at the card and saw she is a director for a centre for women and children . I told her I cannot allow that to happen and that I had to phone my seniors to get that permission and Yvonne who was next to me said she just text  Lelani (residential social worker) and told her what's happening. Lelani phoned me back immediately and told me "if the lady is still there let her take the boys and tell he to bring them back tomorrow so we can sort this thing out with them because it will be no use to  argue now with her . As she won't see reason. The group of boys entered the boys section with a very bad and rude attitude and took our PJs for them for the night and got in the car and we let them leave. I phoned the police and told the police that the group of boys where found. We got the rest of the boys all settled and in bed to sleep.

The next morning around  10am the lady (zulfa) came with the group of boys to meet with our director and social worker. I informed the schools where the boys attended that they won't be at school today because of previous night's incident. We all went to the office whole team and receptionist and we listened to what the lady had to say and what the reason for her taking the boys for the night.
According to her she found the group of boys on vangate drive near to grandwest she recognised one boy  stop her car and call them aside to ask them what they were doing there and they said that Mr Mo (ME) did hit, smack them and chased them with a belt or something to hit them because they didn't do duties. And I allow that the big boys hit them then mr mo just laughs while they are being bullied. So ran away and wanted to go to his mother  (addie) that stay in langebaan where adnaan mom live.

We all just let her speak and tell her side of the
story and then we spoke and told her that the
particular group of boys she is talking about has
been causing problems (shoplifting, stealing,
breaking windows, climbing on roofs and
breaking in by rooms)
And that what they said is not true and nobody
touch or chased them they ran away on their
own accord and the been doing that for a while .
She had a lot to say about our securities in our
premises and it is a danger to let the boys just
slip in and out my director  explained to her
about about the details. But still they didn't see
reason so she left swearing and shouting that she
will report us to the department and we will
hear from him she told that the boys that they
must come to her if they are being treated badly
or bullied and she left.

*The following to days I was off duty at home and when I returned to work on Friday the group of boys did the following*

- *Sleep outside on the premises*
- *Broke the solar panel of the geyser*
- *Broke 4 big windows*
- *Stole money*
- *Broke in the director's office*
- *Did defecate  in the foyer of reception and rubbed in on the windows*
- *And did not attend school they ran on and off the premises*
- *Broke the social worker car back window and urinated on top of the car*

And when the staff reprimanded the group of boys  they ran to the lady (zulfa) then she bought them back and took the boys side and only listen to what they had to say  and not listen to what the staff had to say. And did not list to our staff it was a hell of a week and we made arrangements that she (zulfa) can keep them for a few days and the internal and external agreed to this. Zulfa arrange that they can stay in the centre for two days while I was on duty by the day after she bought them back when she realised that they stole money from her wallet, food from the storage room, broke a few windows and fights with the other children on the premises. When she returned with them we all where call in and she apologised and we accepted her apology and she told the boys not to come to the centre again and we told her that if they come do not open the gates just chase them away.

We as a team we gathered them all in the hall of our centre with the other children and we all let them apologies for what they did to everyone and they saw that we as a team stood united and we all wants what is best for them. Some boys came to apologise individually but they did and we manage to get their bad behaviour in tact We as a team stood united against them. And because of that  the boys couldn't find a way to manipulate staff and let them get their way. Because we stood as a team handling the destruction the boys caused we could support each other and assist when we needed.the importance of working in a team when you are in the lifespace of children is critical that everyone's role is important and understood. There will forever be cases where children try to manipulate or turn staff against one another to get their own ways difficulties that Child and youth care workers face when working with kids is they run off the premises and then whoever they see that they can manipulate and get their way they  will tell you all sad soppy stories they will do it, then these people will come to the centres and come guns blazing ready to argue with the staff of the apparent ill treatment that the children face (children stories - lies) and when some people hear the truth they get a better perception of what we deal with. And the best success in such situation is that the whole staff stick together and tell the truth.

# A Pencil Needs Sharpening.

*A blunt pencil cannot make a proper mark.*

We are all in need of specialized skills and knowledge in our field of expertise. The world is changing very fast and technology is taking over. If you want to be a proper leader, you must sharpen your skills. A wise man once told me that the best way to do this is to read. There are millions of books that will give you information and advice on dealing with certain issues that affect children

- Read up on why children steal
- Bully or fight
- How to deal with stressful situations
- Children behaviour
- Anger management
- Dealing with loss (if parents or family of child passed away)
- ADHD/ADD dealing with  living with
- FAS (fetal alcohol syndromes)
- Disciplining a child

. You can also find information on the internet. There are many professionals in the field that post articles and publish e-books online.

You must be very prepared when you are working with children. Children have a knack for spotting a person who lacks confidence and does not know what they are talking about. You should be excited to be working with them. I also recommend that you use humor. If the children think you are boring, they will lost interest and chaos will ensue. I like to use music, ice breaker activities, dance, and video clips. To sharpen these skills it is important to attend professional development events and classes such as, workshops, forums, and conferences. This will help you stay up to date in the field of youth leadership.

When we started doing developmental programs at our centre I was assigned with the age group 12 to 14 (boys and girls mix) now in group I had two children diagnosed with ADHD, had two with down syndrome and the other where very hyper active kids.  All 12 of them had their own special developmental area which came with challenges. So I was face with doing an activity or facilitate a lesson with them. Nw knowing that they can get very bored easily if i'm just going to talk to them. And most of them cannot write or read properly so how am I going to do this.
Victim empowerment - fire safety
(developmental program)

1. I used music, sound to get them all relax and calm (played a song that they knew and can sing along to)
2. Then I did an icebreaker. (Hot potato always worked for me then music chairs. And a quick simon says)
3. Now knowing the diverse developmental challenges my group has I used video clips from YouTube to get my message across and download a questionnaire from the internet that just require to choose the correct answer.
4. After the video clip I discussed what they have watch and what they learned from watching it from the answers I have compiled from them I can either put
5.  more videos on or start with the questionnaire then we end up with a quick check in
6. I play some music and dona quick icebreaker to burn all access energy.

# A Pencil is Accompanied by an Eraser

Every masterpiece that has ever been created started out with mistakes. There was a mistake made and an eraser was used to correct the mistake. Everyone will make mistakes. It is important to teach children that it is okay to make mistakes, but that when we make a mistake we must learn from it. Through trial and error and inner strength we need to become positive role models for children. We need to show them that adults make mistakes as well, but we are able to learn from our mistakes.

For example, if a child received a low score on an exam, acknowledge the child for partaking in the exam and then support them in reflecting and preparing for the next exam. First, celebrate the score achieved, but then motivate and assist the child in working harder to get a better score. As a leader, we need to teach and model how to handle conflicts when they arise.

I demonstrated this to the children that I lead when I was confronted by a colleague in a very unprofessional manner. I remained calm and let my colleague vent their frustrations and shout at me until they were done. I waited until they walked away and I continued with what the children and I were doing before this incident. When we finished our activity, I went to my colleague and discussed the issue when we could both speak reasonably. Then, she apologised to me and to the kids I lead for her unprofessional behavior. From this, the children learned that it is important to think before speaking and to own their mistakes and apoligise when necessary.

Apologizing is something than many children do not consider often enough. It is our job as a leader to model this action to the children we work with. Children should be taught to apoligise when they recognize they've made a mistake. Children should also be taught that even if they haven't done anything wrong that they can apoligise to avoid conflicts over insignificant matters.

# A Pencil is Reusable

Even if a pencil is worn down to a small bit of wood and lead, it can still make a mark. Even a small, heavily used pencil can start a masterpiece. Remember, as role models we must not give up and think that we are too young or too old to make a difference. No matter your age, appearance, or colour, you can make a difference. Even if it's just sitting and actively listening to a child speak to you, that action can still make a tremendous difference. That conversation could be the beginning of a very positive impact on the life of that child. As they say, "Rome was not built in a day." Even if you have failed a few times- try again. Even if the journey is long, you must continue and persevere.

I worked with children in a residential children's home for five years. In those five years, my perspective changed drastically. I got a glimpse into the life of these children. It made me reflect on, and wonder that what these children went through and how we, as adults, failed them. Then when I come home in my community, I see the children there facing similar challenges. The end result is that these children fall through the cracks end up just another dark statistic of gang war, drugs, prostitution. Or they become another victim of the prison system. When working with children, building a relationship is important. It has to be positive, trusting, professional relationship. On this journey you will learn many things from the children you work with. The children will also teach you many things.

Creating a strong relationship with children will help you guide them through their behavior issues. Some of the behavior issues I dealt with during my time at the children's home were, fist fights, foul language, bullying, destruction of property, defiance, and stealing. Children are bound to exhibit difficult or inappropriate behaviors. I advise you to separate the behavior from the child. Do not label the child as a troublemaker, bully, thief, etc. Instead, emphasize that the behavior was wrong, but that the child is good and capable of improving. For example, if a child is fighting with other children, do not label the child as a bully but say to the child that "you are such a good child, but your behavior is wrong and we cannot fight every time there is a problem." Often, when children misbehave they are testing your response. This can be a method for children to decide if you truly care about them.

There were two times that a child stole from me while I worked at the children's home. I was asked to make a case against the child both times. I decided not to because if I made a case against the child, I would just be giving up on them like so many adults had before. Money can be replaced but a child's trust cannot be so easily replaced.

# Relationship Building and the Three Phases in child and youth care

1. Honeymoon Phase: This is the first phase of the relationship where you and the child will get to know each other on a very basic level. The child will be very reserved and nice to you. This is a phase where everything will go smoothly before the child begins to test you. It's a nice (leka)  period.
2. Testing Phase: During this phase, the child will begin to misbehave. They are testing your reactions and responses to their behaviors. They want to know the boundaries of the relationship.
3. Stability Phase: Then comes a phase where your relationship is predictable, in a sense that the child knows how you will respond to certain behavior. In this phase you must remember to be the adult and do not give up on the child. Continue to try new approaches to the child's misbehaviors.

Relationship Building Phase: During the relationship building phase, take note of the child's strengths and use that to build and maintain a positive relationship. Remember, all behaviors have a purpose. A child has a need to belong. Make a point to get the child involved in groups that give the child a sense of belonging and peer support. You will also want to show the child that you accept them regardless of their individual circumstances. You can do a home visit to demonstrate your acceptance.

## Additional Relationship Building Advice

I remember children whose parents lived on the street and we went to go visit them with the kids. Initially, they were embarrassed, but we ensured them that everything would be okay. We showed the children that we would respect their parents, and families no matter what. We met their parents and hugged and shook hands with them. On our way home the children had a much greater respect for me. It is very beneficial to try to strengthen bonds with the families and the community by means of phone calls, letters, emails and home visit to encourage the child.

Every child is worth saving. Teach them that they are worth it and that they mean something. Teach them skills and build on the skills that they already have. This could be any skill, from soccer, singing and dancing to cooking or building. Encourage the child to improve the skills they already have and help them learn to share their skills with others. Sometimes skills are passed down from relatives that the child learned from through observing their grandparents or parents.

 If you get the chance you should make a point of attending cultural events. For example, you could go to their church, mosque or other African(Zulu, Xhosa, Sotho) cultural  event. It will show support and child will feel more accepted by you. Spiritual upliftment will also boost their self-esteem.

You should also make a point to talk about emotions and find out what the child is feeling. This will help you teach them to identify their emotions and deal with how they are feeling. While you discuss emotions, it can help to reflect the emotions back to the child by summarizing what they have told you. This helps the child create a better internal dialogue.

Teach children to give without expecting
something in return. Teach them to give, help,
and assist others. Doing something like visiting a
nursing home, shelter, or informal settlement
could be an eye-opening experience. They could
hand out bread that they bought or something
that they made for other people to bring them
joy.

# Attitude

When you are working in the life space of a child you must have a positive attitude. The children will pick up on how you are projecting yourself in their space. You must look confident when are with your group and your method of communication must be positively congruent (verbal and non verbal). For instance, if you are standing slumped over and just reading from a page with no emotions and your eye contact is mostly focused on the page, the group you are with will lose interest and start being disruptive. The kids will start doing their own things and entertaining themselves. Children need constant stimulation.

before any specific program that u do with children you need to get them settled. if u are going to do a program that would require u to just stand in front of them explain like a teacher facilitator. motivation talks, career advice or any program that won't require physical movement u need to use ice breakers

When u have an age  group
- 5 - 9 talk less have more activities flashcards, video clips colouring pages .
- 9 - 12 - activities projections flash cards (maybe colouring pages to colour in) depending on developmental age)
- 12 - 16 - activities , interaction, and engage 16 - up - activities, interaction,video clips, worksheets, engage in conversation

 I have found that it helps to begin with an ice breaker activity to get to know the group of children you are working with. The ice breaker should be something that releases energy and gets them to laugh, move around, and have fun. This could be an activity like musical chairs. I also like to include an ice breaker activity that is related to the program I am giving. This helps create a natural transition to the program.

I did a lesson about emotions and the ice breaker activity that I had the children participate in was a game of charades. In this game I asked someone to act out an emotion and the rest of the children would guess which emotion was being acted out. It was important for me to acknowledge everyone's participate as well as make sure that everyone had a chance to participate. When I work with a group of children I prepare myself very thoroughly. I always prepare in a manner where I can explain it to someone much younger than the age group I am working with. I do this so that my program is adaptable for all ages. When I do my program I explain it like I own it, like it's mine. If I use a page, I only use the keywords as a guide. I use reflection and mirror it to the children. It helps to use yourself and the children to explain the program content. Additionally, you must remember the developmental differences of each child. Some will take longer to understand, so you will have to check in with them and pair them with those who were quicker to catch on and ask them to assist the ones in need of help. With this practice you are creating an environment of peer support. The children will feel a strong sense of self-worth. As a result, their self esteem is boosted and the program message is understood.

*** How  I used my attitude** Hike to Cecile waterfalls (hiking trails in Cape Town) (3 hour hike) It was when I was ask to go on a hike with group of children in our centre with Table Mountain Hiking Club Now the morning none of the children wanted to go I had three special needs children with me in the group. I had ADHD and F.A.S diagnosed children and the rest was normal children ages from 14 -18 we were a group of (+-16) The morning of the trip the children where moaning complaining and just didn't feel to go. Even in the bus they were going on and on of not going on the hike wanting to stay in the van and wait for us to return (I also felt the same) but as we approach the hiking trail and met the organizers of the hike the children didn't even smile when the people introduced themselves and the rules. I immediately changed my attitude and energized myself up physically and mentally with some jokes and shouting" woooow we are here  come guys." One by one the children started to warm up. On the trial I cheered them on to them to the fast walkers to the slow one we were met with steep hills narrow path ways downhill climbs, thorns and trees and other obstacles on the hiking trail. The children showed so much teamwork support and guided helped each other. I made it fun I was present with them everyone was there they laughed cheered each other on supportive and was patient with each other (specially with the special needs children) they would wait for each other keep hands do check ins with each other. Conversations where going and there was team building amongst them. When we came ontop to take a break and watch the beautiful view I had a talk with the group - I ask them how does the view look from atop and they said it looks beautiful "mooi meneer yoh kyk da en kyk net die see en dit" pointing out to different scenery that was eye catching to them (life through the eye of a child ) and then a questioned them * was it easy for them to get till here they responded no sir ( nee meneer ) the hills where steep somewhere narrow . We walk through thorny bushes and some downhill steep (yoh die heuwels and doring bosses and dai nou padjie was swaar) was difficult. * if we gave up by the first steep hill would we see this view - children said no (nee meneer waar ) we won't we will just be seeing the trees and cars roads at the bottom *now I explain to them that this is what life is all about forever there will be obstacle in our life some easy some difficult to overcome but if u are confident and motivate yourself you will achieve anything u set out (goals). Like u mention if we stopped we would only see trees cars and roads in front of u that will be the same when u decide to give up and don't want to try harder will just stay there and your vision for yourself will be block cuts and bruises knocks and bumps heartache and pain is life way of acknowledge achievement so whatever we face ahead of us from this point onwards we face it head on strong and determine to overcome. Then we acknowledge our victory with some refreshments and hand claps gestures and smiles.

 A highlight of the day was we came across a steep hill one of the children (special needs) had some difficulty to come up and one of the boys and a guide (table mountain hiking club) wants to help her and she said no no I can and she climbed that steep hill while the rest of us cheered her on and clapped shouting her name. The facial expression she had.

The confident and her whole body language changed when she reached the top With this simple exercise I used observation skills,my communication skills (verbal and nonverbal) my energy, humor my attitude and Patients I learned a lot from the kids and they learned from me there was a lot of sharing caring and teamwork


*if I had to have a negative attitude and wasn't looking confident and didn't use humor on this trip I do believe that the end result for the day would have been way different (fighting, swearing, moaning and complaining) So when u work with kids remember positive attitude.

# Be the Adult

You will come across challenging behaviors where you will be pushed beyond your limits of patience and remaining calm. And u will at times lose your temper in some forms whether its shouting. Screaming and behave unprofessionally, the children will push you. (Like throwing petrol on a fire) You as the person in the child's life  space u must always be aware  of what triggers you  name calling - when u have big ears, or nose or anything that looks different the children will tell u straight out and if it triggers u they will continue to use it as means to get u angry

* Remember children behavior comes with a need Swearing

- children that u work with will continuously swear and they will swear at you but not at you ( they swearing at your title)

Stealing- they know no boundaries they will take things without asking some will literally break in to steal things
they were never taught any boundaries by their parents so respecting other people's personal space and boundaries is a challenge for them

Inappropriate behaviors - children will act out by ignoring you, not doing chores. Fight, bullying

* now u as the adult must remember respond do not react to these kinds of behavior. - think before u do And if it comes where u feel that u have boiling point take time out and ask for assistance from someone else

. Try a different approach to the children's behavior when they test you Read facial expressions and body language of your children -

e.g child that greeted u every day when they come from school and is always active in your programs/session with them and on a particular day he/she just storm pass you room and has aggressive behavior towards others. - if u go to that child and say to him  come get done we going start soon u will get a bad a negative reaction from that child.

In my experience I gave the child time to get undress and eat and say to everyone loud that we will start soon with our program/session keeping in mind child's earlier behavior and continue when everyone is present. Start with my ice breaker and continue with my program/session but also observing the child and monitor his/her participation (body language. Facial expressions) and make a mental note have a conversation with him about what happened that he behaved in this manner. With this u strengthen the relationship with the child and the child will start to trust u more and will feel a sense of belonging.

# Being in the life space of a child

Lifespace work is where u must think on your *feet and be able to use whatever u have at your* disposal to use to facilitate a learning session Working in the moment Working at the moment in the space of a child when u focus on that between in between moments of everyday routine. It is that moments that we as workers miss out on and it is these moments that is usable in doing life space work Sometime we as workings we are so overwhelmed with work and getting things done that we miss out on these opportunities to use these moments. When u present and observant of the child u will start seeing strength based qualities that is hidden in all that chaotic behavior .and when u notice these strengths and good qualities of behavior in the child. It will be easy to meet the desired need behind the behavior (with every behavior comes a need) with such an approach u will focus more on the child's behavior and not on the child (all children are special) Using a child strength as a means as to build relationship . Eg a child is a good soccer player but insulting, teasing  ( and bullies younger kids. Now when u are present and observant u can use the good soccer qualities to work on the behavior Approach the child and mention his strength. U are such a good soccer player (strength) why don't u teach the younger boys to play as well as u. But if you agree we must work together and be supportive with them and no bullying and fighting on the field. With this approach the child learned a new skill sense of belonging Sharing , supporting. Generous Confident and more in control of himself remember to do with the children

# <u>Stimulation</u>

When working with children u will learn that they need constant stimulation or something to keep them busy, because when all that access energy built up and they end up being bored and frustrated they start getting agitated and angry with each other and that's when fidgeting and poking, name calling starts happening and in most times it end up with a fight and lots of swearing. Now one thing that people uses is come lets watch a movie

Which is a good way to use if it age appropriate and not boring where u can also use to message good qualities and bring a message across

Be careful when choosing movies for children keep in mind age groups because movies sometimes

display sexual behavior

Inappropriate dressing

Language ( bad mouth. Swearing)

Fighting (bullying) Even cartoons have hidden subliminal messages that is design for kids brains.

Eg. Ben 10 when he is confronted by adults be throws a tantrum and turn into a monster to get his way * child might learn that throwing tantrums can be a way of getting my way and at times when children watch tv/movies they get bored energy build up and it ends up with fights swearing teasing My experience I was faced many times with these dilemmas and type is behavior and what I realized is when the movie end children is more energies and cannot fall asleep (ADHD diagnosed kids seems they are more active) and it caused difficulties during sleeping time (movies was only watch on weekends) So I used energy releasing activities and games that I played with the children before we go watch movie/tv and some of the activities are such fun and it releases so much build up energy from u and we learn and teach each other - when u participate in playing with the children they see u in a different capacity they feel more relax and it is also an opportunity to use to bond strengthen relationship

## Work on strength .

Give sense of belonging and building on skills

Here are a few games that I used and it is adaptable to play in any conditions indoor or outdoors

Wolf Wolf hoe laat is dit(Wolf wolf what time is it)


Kennetjie - hand and eye coordination
Niekies - memory ( os was altyd a klomp en hulle regte name en score)
3 blikkies 3 cans - hand and eye coordination and to work under pressure king king - hand eye coordination and to work your frustration out constructively
Aan aan met a tennis ball (tag/your it ) - hand eye coordination and stress verlos
Hide and seek - fit and good memory
Hand tennis - strategic planning and coordination
Hokke (Hopscotch) - coordination kept me physical phitness
Skipping Rope – Rhythm and beat, physically fit
3 Sticks – physically fit and strategic jumping

And some of these games the kids know and have games that they played when they were at home when they were younger When u play with them their game they get confident. They get a chance to lead. They teaching a new skills, energy gets burn and most importantly everyone is having fun. *tips even if u are not active in sport or able to run participate in the game. While u there and play with them game they will continue with the game. Gives u a chance to use your observation skills to for developmental areas in the child

**WHAT I LEARNED FROM THESE GAME**
It's kept me physically fit,
I learned about time
It though me to run if a stranger comes after you
(Wolf wolf)
Leadership skills
burned energy
Fun
Stimulating
Memory Skills

# DOING WITH THEM (EXPERIENTIAL LEARNING/ LEARNING THROUGH EXPERIENCE)

When working with children/youth you will come. Be in their life space and have to be doing activities, outing with them to keep them busy. And the best way to plan is to them in the process of planning.

My experience On many occasions I take my group of boys out on a outing to mark occasions such as birthdays, new child coming to our group or exciting.

We would sit together planned a date (all events I plan on my of days) and I take it forward to the team (senior child care worker, social worker, director) and they agree. I urge boys to save from there own pocket money for extra luxuries (they do) We get our stuff in order and I set a behavior agreement with them if duties is not done according to rooster. Name is in the incident report Homework program attendants Or any misbehavior I will move it till u guys can fully cooperate and work as a team

On the day of the outing The Saturday morning
we get breakfast and we sit together and I put
money on the table (always keep some aside)
and tell them we going to Seapoint beach (they
decided) so here is the money work out our
cheapest of traveling (taxi or train) let them
decide.
 Boys decided on train we can walk to the station
take the train to cape town and walk to sea point
we can spend time in Greenpoint park and walk
up till sea point pavilion (group decision - I
always make sure everyone in the group agrees)
Then we walk to the nearest station buy tickets
and have random talks about everything under
the sun (from pass events, what they did at
home ect.)

And I listen attentively to what they say and
mental notes of things that I need to follow up
on

*always be present*

We take mini races from one point to another (burns energy children are excited) And let the children lead the way ask them what road to take next ( giving everyone a time to lead) and I encourage them if we get lost we get lost together. As we get to the station I explain to them that I don't want them to stand by the trains doors and the dangers and we must always stick together when we walking. When we come to cape town I get a place where we can group up in a circle and we discuss money We need to eat, drink and travel home I let them decide to break in the groups and decide who buys what food and chips and drinks. (Always put u ideas also on the table -but let them decide) - to direct them in a more realistic way of thinking example come we buy gatsbys, chips, drinks and sweet or buy fish and chips parcel and use the rest of the money to buy drink and chips the the final decision must be there you as the adult are just there to guide them to make an informed choice. Now after they decide the groups I put the question on the table with the amount of money we have "guys u can either take money and go with your team and go buy the stuff or go check the prices of the stuff come back and we work out the budget. The reason being is some of u might have more and some of u might have less so decide. Boys decided that they will do the price check first and come back we worked out a budget and actually bought more stuff than what they intend and had changeleft. they  were surprised, happy and proud and what they achieved, they where excited and laughed   (facial expression was priceless from the kids) Then we decide to work and boys ask can we maybe drink one cool drink on the way and we did on our walk from cape town we had the silliest, funniest, intellectual conversations under the sun.

When boys ask can we go play here and I get up there my response was go be children and of you get hurt (scrape your knee, a knock or anything small) remember life is not smooth sailing u will get knocks scrapes and get hurt so don't cry cos the decision to climb and jump was yours. (Nothing dangerous - we came across a few parks on the way . When we came pass Greenpoint park I said to boys our furthest point will be by the pool where we will swim and play eat so we can either come play here (Greenpoint park) on our way back and they said fine. And we walked up to sea point pavilion. swimming pool and had an awesome day. On our way back when we reached Greenpoint park and children played some time we grouped together and discussed the days happening and how it was what was learned and where can we improve.Now as we sit together I open a bag of chips and say these words "With this bag of chips I am opening I am welcoming u to the new venture u enduring we will  forget what happen in the past and focus on getting stronger wiser and to make more inform decisions. So as we pass the chips around mention a good quality of each other and what your day was like. And we pass the around each one saying something positive and good then I give them a few minutes to play. Then we continue our journey I ask a few boys to go buy ice cream for us (the extra money I had) and we walk to cape town

and put them in a taxi and give them taxi fare
home and I go home.

With such this I have gave them

Sense of belonging - group felt they belong they
are part of something, they feel important
Skills - they learned time management,
budgeting,
Generosity - learned to share, care for each other
Independence- being in control of emotions.
Doing things alone.
 Self esteem - child feels they are worthed , they
feel confidant and that he can achieve


## Self care

When working with children/youth we are so
overwhelmed with work we forget about our
self and lose our self in the process. And this is
the reason we reach boiling point and put
ourself out. When we feel like this we stress get
frustrated angry and our interaction is
unproductive with the group and we feel
despondent and feel that whatever we do is so
useless and will start blaming others.

we feel despondent because we are not effective in working with the children, we feel so overwhelmed with emotions and stress that we get angry quickly and take our frustrations out on either on our colleagues or the children in our care. taking self care is a vital thing to de when working with children. It gives u time to work on yourself and re-energise.

*conference session care for the carers (break away session) I attend an biannual conference

- story of two sisters arishni and Vernish was sisters that grew up together and had a close bond with each other, but as time grew on they also have grown apart each one taking on a different venture of their own Arishni was more into artificial things everything must look perfect lavish then see is good. Whenever she was faced with emotion she will build or make something beautiful instead of dealing with what she felt Vernish was more in caring and worrying about others she was more in touch with her emotions and worried about how and what others feel now as time went by the both moved away from each other each one building a life of its own. Now both of them started to have less and less contact until there was no contact with each other at all one particular day Arishni felt something is missing and she build everything lavish and good but cant find why she feels empty and she tried to fill it up by buying and building more around the place but the emptiness was still there. She became frustrated, angry sweared and was just short tempered with anyone and everyone. She then decided ill go visit my sister it's been a while since we had any contact with each other. She prepared her journey and went with her guards to her sisters place. As she reached her sisters place. She was stopped by guards asking her why she is her and she explains that she is here to see her sister. The guards called one of the helpers of the sister to ask if she will accept the visit. The sister accepts the visit Upon entering she noticed it's cold she was showed the direction of where her sisters chambers are . On the road till there she was stopped by guards that told her *only u Arishni may enter from here on your guards have to wait her. She agreed. And continued with her journey and was stopped by a different guard  said no bags from this point on or go back and she continued. Met with different guards till she was completely naked .*

*She start to notice that the place look dark, cold and empty started to feel a chill run down her spine and wondered why the place look so unkept. Her sister (Vernish) grabbed her and tied her to a chain and beat scratch and hurt her. Arishni screamed in agony and pain. Vernish looked dark like a possessed demon and when she looked in the eyes of Vernish she just saw hatred pain anger fear. She pleaded and shouted for help but the torture continued. Until the little helpers came all running to her aid, but they had to handle the situation delicately so what they did is they start shouting oh no her eyes look at the beauty in that eyes it's going to be taken away. He arm look at the strength in her arm if u continue to torcher it will be taken away They continue to identify parts of her and the torcher stopped. Arishni ask Vernish please let me go I can't take this pain, Vernish agreed but on one condition that the pathway between us stays open and with regular visits. They both agree and lived together in harmony and Arishni emptiness was fulfilled Vernish place brightened and became more alive and warm*

# What I have learned from this

When your brain and heart work together and agree you are more in touch with feeling and emotion. -how to achieve this is as simple as

- Reading - books. Short stories, novels
- Friends- go visit old friend, make new friends socialize fun
- Go watch a movie
- Make jokes
- Exercise - go for short walks. Hikes or simple exercise
- Treat yourself - go for dinner, massage holiday, beach
- Journal - write down your feelings identify, your triggers, write down challenges faced during the day, write down highlights of the day.
- Talk- talk to a close friend, senior worker, or a mentor, any trusting person in your life.

- Even during your work period take a moment in your busy day and have coffee with the rest of the workers and have conversation, share the day with them ask advice on difficulty faced during the day and mention highlights of the day no matter how small it may seem.

# Bonding

When we work with children we are required to bond and build strong positive relationship which might sound easy but its not.

 The children that we work with comes from a history of being let down by adults or adults used them just for gaining purpose. So in their eyes we as adults are the enemy and we just want from them, and when we done we will leave them and the pain will come again
. So in order for them to deal with the pain they act out, manipulate and behave inappropriately at times. My experience. I used everyday day moments in our daily routine our centre to bond with the children in the centre.

Meal times randomly I will ask the youth the help me dish up food for the rest of the children I ask one to dish up and I will dish the rice and there is more around I will just supervise and delegate who does what. One dish food one dish rice One dish salad a group set table (forks on each one place) Meals on the table group does that At first they will say I can't "nee meneer ek kanie - Afrikaans " then I will respond neither can I "ek kan oek nie -  Afrikaans " And. Then I will say u can't I cant well then we all will learn today because  tomorrow you are at home and will be ask to dish up or are u going to wait for me cos I wont be around forever. Then the kids will dish up and they dish up perfectly (sometimes better than me) and during this time we converse over anything that happened during the day at school or past. After we done we call the others and we sit down and eat and continue have conversation

 (sometimes it gets noisy but its children - be the adult speak respectively when u want them to speak softer) then according to the rooster kitchen duties must get done

# <u>Routines</u>

When working with children you will notice that they are at times anxious over things and have certain behavior traits when it comes to meal times and so on. ( children hide food, cannot fall asleep, ect) now reason for this is that they usually had to fend for themselves and a simple thing as sleeping time or the next meal was a constant uphill battle, not knowing when and where will the next meal or sleeping time be. Now to ease this pressure from a child and make the child more relaxed and at ease. A routine in the daily life of a child. will ease the stress anxiety on the child and he will become more relaxed and behavior patterns will change, because now the child will become accustomed to the sequence of the day knowing what will follow next after each program/activity. And with a structured routine building relationship or strengthening your relation with child/group

And this is when u work with the child between the in-between moments of daily life routine. With the child participation u can design a well structured routine that can be flexible in case of unforeseen circumstances it doesn't have to be iron grid but.

* at the centre where I worked our routine was as follows

5:30. - wake up and get ready for school
6: 30 - breakfast
6: 45 - 730- school transport drop of

__________________

13:30 - 14:30 children come from school
14:30 - 15:00 lunch is serve
15:00 - 15: 45 free time
15:45 - 16:00 exercise
16:00 - 17: 00 developmental programs/home
work
17:00 - 18:00 bath time & duties
18:00 - 19:00 supper and duties 1
9 :00 - 19: 45 free time
20 : 15 Quiet time & check in/virtues

Virtues are the essence of our character and
character does indeed determine destiny. The
more we recognize the potential impact that
practicing *virtues* can have on our lives, the more
our lives open up to new possibilities and to
greater joy and fulfillment

List a few of virtues we did in our program at our centre, we would be given one virtue and explain it to the. and discussed how they understand it. One virtue over a two week period per virtue

I would gather the children that is in my care and we all would sit in the room. then I would ask question say we do Respect. Now I would read about respect to the children and then ask them what they understand.
i would get answer like respect is greeting someone with a smile, respect is using words like excuse me, may I please have this, knocking on a door before entering, not swearing, some will say giving your seat for a elderly person when u sit in a bus.
I would then ask with what previous virtue does respect also come in they would answer from virtues we did. sometimes I would divide them in groups two groups and ask them to do a short act on how to show respect and the other group do a scene without respect then we have then tell us what was the scene about and where was respect shown and where was it not  shown.
- Self-discipline
- Compassion
- Responsibility
- Friendship
- Courage
- Perseverance

- Honesty
- Loyalty
- Faith.
- Respect
- Love
- Creativity

20: 30 sleeping time

Check in is just you as a worker asking a child how his/her day was doing any highlight of the day and what can we improve in your day and with this the child feels that u are interested in his daily life they feel listened to and the feel worthed a check - in can be like hey

Worker : how was your day john
John : its was nice
Worker : what was so nice of your day
John: well sir/mam at school I did...
Worker so it sounded like u had a day so if u in the group of children get everyone to participate in talking.

 Make notes on what conversation u need to follow up on, report to social worker. Look at facial expressions. Check in times before bed times must be done in a manner where the child does not expect it, it must not be a formal thing they must feel relax and guard must be done.

# <u>Make it yours</u>

When working with children make moments magical and make moments count and make it yours. Adapt s beat or a lyric or a time in the daily routine that is entirely you and your child/children's time where u guys do things your way together .


* At our centre we worked shifts now every second Sunday when I was on duty I call the boys together and we did was the bedding of our room. We will divide the groups in teams like this group
strip the beds,
 group to sweep the room,
a group to wash,
hang and take of the washing when dried.

The boys clean and pack cupboards and short out school bags and clothes and all dirty clothes we wash out. When bedding and clothes are done as a collective the group make the beds and present to me with school clothes and bags for the week.

With this the children learn skills, develop a team work, and feel more confident and that they belong and are worth and mean something. It also give u time to have conversation and find out what's happening within the group/child (animosity, fights, feuds) and get it sorted out just there and find a manner to get the group to be working in harmony with each other. *children tend to take each other things or use each other stuff * jealous amongst each other * name calling and whatever is happening in the group can and must be sorted out

## Making moments count.

We went to different workshops and one workshop. They spoke about lollipop moments lollipop moments .(video clip)

*So this guy talks about how he get a in invite to a wedding of a girl he has connection with and any recollection of meeting he tried to remember search and search his memory box. He finally met up with with this girl and ask her how she knows him and this is what she said. It was on the day of her colleges/varsity registration and she was nervous as hell, shaking in her boats anxious and anxiety of how a student feel when entering a college/varsity. And u (this guy) had a funniest looking hat ever seen handing out lollipops to random people in the line, then u gave one to a anxious looking guy in front of me(the guy i'm marrying) and told him to give to me and when u accept it u told my parents "look their not even away from home yet and she is taking candy from a stranger" but u are right where I need to be. And it is at that moment I felt relax and calm and confident knowing exactly that this is where my new journey in life start, that this moment counts that it's going to be now. And with that moment with your words it made me feel more confident and calm. Your words inspired me, your words gave me strength to carry on.*

Now with this extract u can read that little moments in our life that goes unnoticed
 Its is small moments happen in your life in our lives that we easily forget
. Everyone has had a lollipop moment if you search your memory banks u will come across many moments when u had a lollipop moment.

***My lollipop moment (child in my care)**When working with children at times we come so overwhelmed with things and sometimes things get to much for us. Our personal life and the stress of the work it gets to much for us. On a particular day I was stressed angry and very much upset. My mind was somewhere else and I was at work (not present) So kids came from school undress and ate. A few was outside playing and I supervised them, so one of the girls in the centre came to me and stood in front of me and ask me"are u ok (is meneer ok) because u don't look ok (want meneer lyk nie ok nie) but u must not  worry it will be ok (moet nie worry nie meneer it gaan raak better raak) can I give sir a hug ( kan ek meneer a drukkie gee) which she did and she walked of and when to go play and hang with her friends. That moment when the child came and I was not myself, when she hugged me and just said it will get better I felt better I felt that even as much as I care for the children they care about me. And even though I don't work with her directly me being here at the centre means something to her. I felt much better. Uplifted and energized. Now as u can see simple words that inspired us as a person to go on, to not give up, to be able to achieve. Acknowledge these moments. Acknowledge the people that created the moment sometimes even they need inspiration. I did however acknowledge her and thank her for that moment which for her was nothing but for me something

# Lollipop moment with a colleague

 I was still new to working in the centre and I was the youngest, the only male child and youth care worker and the one with high energy levels always active and ready to do something

Now on this particular day me and one lady that works with me in the boys section had abit of an outfall and we exchange words with each other. The one thing she said to me was you mean nothing here  "jy is niks werd hier  nie" and that words struck me hard and it hurt it made me angry, furious I was so bewildered by anger that I wanted to leave just there at that moment and give up just walk away get something else to do. So I walked up to another colleague (team leader) and I ask her can I talk to her and she dropped everything she was busy with and told me come we go at the back I also need a smoke break (workers not allowed to smoke in front of children) so we went and I explain to her what happen and how I felt and that I feel I must go how do I write my resignation letter so I can leave. She did let me vent and talk let out all my frustrations without interrupting me one moment.

When I was done she said well u can give up
and just walk away and leave I can help u write
your resignation letter. But why don't u use this
moment to shine why don't u show her that u
can achieve and that u are worthy use this as a
means to grow because we see your interaction
with the children and u connect with children
that we found difficult to.

 We see your strength and the children here
needs u, use this to show them u can u don't
need her do what u need to do to keep yourself
covered. And go make amends with your
colleague u had an argument with say (both of u
weren't behaving like adults) I was the first to
apoligise and we became better workers and yes
we had other arguments but that will happen
but what matters is saying sorry and move on
We stood for a while in silence and came back
inside continued with the day. That night I laid
and thought about it and decided I can do it.

 And with those few words that moment that she
made time for me to talk to her. That moment
she left what she was doing (she had lots to do)
to listen to me it gave me myself back and I felt
that I can and I won't give up. From that
moment on me and her had a great bond we still
do.

We talk and shared ideas and I always reminded and reminds her of what that moment meant for me. (She just smiles and will always say Mo ( my name they called me) I love u) And even though that moment meant nothing it meant something to me. It mattered to me it counted if it wasn't for that moment I might have taken a different path but here I am now.

# <u>Identity (culture)</u>

A child's culture is part of his identity it is where he belongs and where he comes from, and some cultures have certain traits that come along with it. And these traits has value and meaning for a child. And if we ignore a child culture we are robbing him of his identity , because thats where he belongs (sense of belonging) And some traits we as a society look pass and sometimes these traits is an insult to our culture and believe and it makes us feel insulted
Eye contact - in some culture a child is not allowed to maintain eye contact with adults it's a sign of disrespect
Dress code - some culture women are not allow to dress in pants (Xhosa, Zulu, Zulu, Venda - African Cultures)
 Decision- some culture the man/father makes all decision regarding his family.

But when working with children u must be culturally aware and at times respect and accept the child's culture.

Best way to gain culture competency is by :
Reading - books on different culture
Child background report
Engaging - talk to people in your community workplace about their culture

Religious/cultural gatherings- attend events and engage with people ask question.
Research - different culture/religions

Our centre

 At the centre I worked at we came up with an idea to have a cultural day for our children.
We pitched the idea to management which they agreed and went had a meeting with all the children in the centre to identify different culture and we chose for out of the cultures that was mentioned.
Cultures was associated with food (through eyes of a child)
Coloured (Cape town) - Gatsbys and Chip Rolls - Consist of a foot long roll fill with a bed of salad, chips(fries)  and a filling of choice such as steak, chicken, polony, vienna, egg, and sauce
Xhosa - pap and vleis  (Pap & Meat) - Maize meal and meat stew
Islam- Roti and Curry - it's a wrap made out of flour salt and oil baked and with mince curry
Portuguese - fish and chips - a piece of snoek and fries
Swedish volunteers and they made meatballs and some Swedish dessert chocolate balls   - meatballs chocolate balls which consist of oatmeal, sugar, cocoa, butter and a small amount of coffee

We the child and youth care workers told the groups they should go do research on the cultures ( food, dance. Clothes. Where it comes from) We invited parents and some of the community members to come and enjoy the day with us. The children did everything required with us workers as guides to them . The event was a success and children made the most of it and got their sense of identity.

When u become culturally aware u will realize that and learn reason being why certain children behave in certain ways. Meal times - some children would want to use their hand - dining room setting - conversation/silence Dress code - some children won't want to wear certain clothing Praying - some would pray at home/church/mosque or do not believe we as worker must accept the child believe and values on work with children to find their true identity

WHAT IS ADHD? ADHD STANDS FOR ATTENTION
DEFICIT HYPERACTIVITY DISORDER. IT IS A MEDICAL
CONDITION. A PERSON WITH ADHD HAS DIFFERENCES
IN BRAIN DEVELOPMENT AND BRAIN ACTIVITY THAT
AFFECT ATTENTION, THE ABILITY TO SIT STILL, AND
SELF-CONTROL. ADHD CAN AFFECT A CHILD AT
SCHOOL, AT HOME, AND IN FRIENDSHIPS.

# What Are the Signs of ADHD?

All kids struggle at times to pay attention, listen
and follow directions, sit still, or wait their turn.
But for kids with ADHD, the struggles are
harder and happen more often.

Kids with ADHD may have signs from one, two,
or all three of these categories:

- **Inattentive.** Kids who are inattentive
  (easily distracted) have trouble focusing
  their attention, concentrating, and staying
  on task. They may not listen well to
  directions, may miss important details,
  and may not finish what they start. They
  may daydream or dawdle too much. They
  may seem absent-minded or forgetful,
  and lose track of their things.

- **Hyperactive.** Kids who are hyperactive are fidgety, restless, and easily bored. They may have trouble sitting still, or staying quiet when needed. They may rush through things and make careless mistakes. They may climb, jump, or roughhouse when they shouldn't. Without meaning to, they may act in ways that disrupt others.
- **Impulsive.** Kids who are impulsive act too quickly before thinking. They often interrupt, might push or grab, and find it hard to wait. They may do things without asking for permission, take things that aren't theirs, or act in ways that are risky. They may have emotional reactions that seem too intense for the situation.

Sometimes parents and teachers notice signs of ADHD when a child is very young. But it's normal for little kids to be distractible, restless, impatient, or impulsive — these things don't always mean that a child has ADHD.

Attention, activity, and self-control develop little by little, as children grow. Kids learn these skills with help from parents and teachers. But some kids don't get much better at paying attention, settling down, listening, or waiting. When these things continue and begin to cause problems at school, home, and with friends, it may be ADHD.

## How Is ADHD Diagnosed?

**If you think your child has ADHD, make an appointment with your child's doctor.** He or she will give your child a check-up, including vision and hearing, to be sure something else isn't causing the symptoms. The doctor can refer you to a child psychologist or psychiatrist if needed.

To diagnose ADHD, doctors start by asking about a child's health, behavior, and activity. They talk with parents and kids about the things they have noticed. Your doctor might ask you to complete checklists about your child's behavior, and might ask you to give your child's teacher a checklist too.

After gathering this information, doctors diagnose ADHD if it's clear that:

- A child's distractibility, hyperactivity, or impulsivity go beyond what's usual for their age.
- The behaviors have been going on since the child was young.
- Distractibility, hyperactivity, and impulsivity affect the child at school and at home.
- A health check shows that another health or learning issue isn't causing the problems.

Many kids with ADHD also have learning problems, oppositional and defiant behaviors, or mood and anxiety problems. Doctors usually treat these along with the ADHD.

## How Is ADHD Treated?

Treatment for ADHD usually includes:

- Medicine. This activates the brain's ability to pay attention, slow down, and use more self-control.
- **Behavior therapy.** Therapists can help kids develop the social, emotional, and planning skills that are lagging with ADHD.
- **Parent coaching.** Through coaching, parents learn the best ways to respond to behavior difficulties that are part of ADHD.
- **School support.** Teachers can help kids with ADHD do well and enjoy school more.

The right treatment helps ADHD improve. Parents and teachers can teach younger kids to get better at managing their attention, behavior, and emotions. As they grow older, kids should learn to improve their own attention and self-control.

**When ADHD is not treated, it can be hard for kids to succeed.** This may lead to low self-esteem, depression, oppositional behavior, school failure, risk-taking behavior, or family conflict.

## What Can Parents Do?

If your child is diagnosed with ADHD:

- **Be involved.** Learn all you can about ADHD. Follow the treatment your child's health care provider recommends. Keep all recommended appointments for therapy.
- **Give medicines safely.** If your child is taking ADHD medicine, always give it at the recommended time and dose. Keep medicines in a safe place.
- **Work with your child's school.** Ask teachers if your child should have an IEP. Meet often with teachers to find out how your child is doing. Work together to help your child do well.

- **Parent with purpose and warmth.** Learn what parenting approaches are best for a child with ADHD — and which can make ADHD worse. Talk openly and supportively about ADHD with your child. Focus on your child's strengths and positive qualities.
- **Connect with others for support and awareness.** Join a support organization for ADHD to get updates on treatment and other information.

## What Causes ADHD?

It's not clear what causes the brain differences of ADHD. There's strong evidence that ADHD is mostly inherited. Many kids who have ADHD have a parent or relative with it.

ADHD is *not* caused by too much screen time, poor parenting, or eating too much sugar.

ADHD can improve when kids get treatment, eat healthy food, get enough sleep and exercise, and have supportive parents who know how to respond to ADHD.

Above reference (http://kidshealth.org/en/parents/adhd.html)

# My experience

In my care was a boy named Stuart he was around 11 years old when I started working at Heatherdale children's home. I was to oversee the room that Stuart was in. In the morning he was the most everywhere and restless up and down. he will tease all children, want to do everything but nothing gets completed everything is simply unfinished from making his bed to getting dress and ready for school. At the time I was still new to Child and youth care, so in my head I was hell what's wrong with this boy he works on my nerves because he  and make me tired.he takes up most of my time and when I get done with him I am so stressed and angry and he I smiling and laughing playing running around. Every morning when he wakes up it's like a uphill battle to get him to go to the bathroom and wash his face, brush his teeth, make his bed and get ready for school before breakfast time, and when I'm done with him my patience is up and then the rest of the kids gets rushed and shouted to get done.then we have breakfast now all children sit together in the dining area at meal times. now 60 children together in the morning stuart is up and down every where teasing any person from child to a workers I had to stop many morning fights because of how he provokes children. there were days I had to run around the centre after him to get dress for school and we always have to look for something like a white shirt for school,  pencil, a book, a shoe a sock, then the transport arrives to take the kids to school and when he is in the van he is the most restless the teasing swearing provoking never stopped till he is dropped of at school.

After school at 13H00 he is the most calm relax
boy ever, he assist and is always helpful, does
whatever u ask him to do whether it is duties or
helping a child and youth care worker with a
task he is there to assist.I notice that around
15H30 he starts getting restless and the
provoking starts. At 16h00 hours it's our
homework time and he never has homework my
colleagues suggested I give him pages to colour
in to keep them busy so I did that, then he will
calmly sit and colour in the page and does it so
beautifully. but when he was done he was back
to being restless and then its up down, on top of
the tables, teasing and name calling, breaking up
fight and running around. and that continued till
he fall asleep.  It was my first month that I was
working at the heatherdale so I was
overwhelmed and stressed when I came home
from work after my shift I just slept.

I had a meeting with our residential social worker and she informed me that she knows about this behaviour patterns and that he is diagnosed with ADHD when I asked why is he like a different type of person when he comes from school she explained to me that it's the medication that he takes Ritalin 20mg which last about 8 hours, I told her that is there any way that we could increase it for longer because his behaviour is a problem after school a meeting was schedule with his doctor we invited the teacher and it was decided to increase it to 30 mg I research more about ADHD/ADD and became more proactive with dealing with him. I worked out a plan that when he comes from school I will get him to sort his bag out for the following day, school clothes and let him was out his school socks to keep him busy, while I tend to the other children and get them to do it also.

while I go through his bag we talk about homework, favourite subjects and what subjects he do not like, funny to say he likes maths. and he finish his homework in class. I then started download math question sheets from the internet and added word search and then I used a colouring in page from one of his favourite cartoon character as a reward, then he will sit with that math sheet and word search pages till he finds all the words and he does it the fastest in the centre so for me homework time till bedtime was sorted with something constructive to do.

during our interaction I found out that he likes music Justin Bieber - baby baby  Chris Brown - superhuman and other songs so with in the morning to get him ready for school before I wake them up I play his favourite song and other songs that the kids like and they will sing and get ready now he is always up and down then I would say if u don't control yourself (it's not easy task for ADHD diagnosed child) I will not play your song and I will monitor him, and when he is done I would ask him to assist the younger children in the section to get ready for school while me and my colleague get the cleaning chemicals ready for the bathroom and toilet to be cleaned according to the duty rooster. During my time working at heatherdale me and stuart build a stronger relationship when he turned 12 years old he moved in to my group and I was indirect care of him,
Because I understood him and had some knowledge about ADHD/ADD dealing with his difficult behaviour was not much of a challenge and I made him understand that ADHD/ADD does not cover for bad behaviour.

I started noticing all his strengths that he had, singing, drawing, his kindness and how creative he was in telling stories or making up songs with his own lyrics, when I approach him and I used his strength based approach with him I could keep him more incontrol of his impulses, he would come and tell me that he needs a wordsearch or math page, then there times we would just toss a ball to each other and talk about what's going on at school and what's on his mind. Yes we had our difficult times when he was not incontrol of himself especially at times when he was phoning his mom and she would promise to come visit the saturday and never pitch up or phone again, then he express his emotions by breaking windows and fighting with anyone But with understanding him we could work out a plan for him on how to control his anger like walking away and sit alone, ask me if u can go lay in your bed, talk to someone how u feeling to avoid the negative outburst. And it worked for us. He improved in school, and was more organised and had more  control with expressing his emotion, especially with his anger

## Difficulty

When you work with children that is diagnosed with ADHD/ADD there is one critical rule in planning a routine for their daily planning it is to be consistent with the structure to your routine that u have worked out for the child, and everyone in the team must work together and stick to the scheduled routine that was planned out for the day for the child. If on the schedule and activity is set to happen it has to happen and if it cannot happen due to circumstances then at have a backup activity planned out to do. example on your routine you have scheduled a soccer match for the day at 16h00 and it rains on that particular day then have an activity for them to do in its place. When u wake up children and u schedule their wake up time is at a  set time the whole team must stick to the time that was set for waking up. the routine must be followed to the last letter and followed consistently and when u make changes to the routine than before u implement the changes have a discussing with the whole team about the changes in the routine and why it works for you.

Being consistent makes the child feel more relaxed and he will start getting used to the sequence of the routine, and with a structured routine it makes disciplining the child easier and with the child's input, you can start seeing the child's strength and abilities and together work out his Independent **Developmental Plan.**

What difficulty comes with this is when the child goes home to his parents, host parents for holidays and they do not follow the structured routined that u had planned out with the child, when the child comes back to the centre you as a worker has difficulty getting the child back into the rhythm of doing things according to the routine, the child  feels confused and stressed, because he just came back from a free open plan routine where he as sleep and took meds when he wanted to and now back at the centre he has to follow a structured routine which is difficult because now the child challenge the worker again and there is more than one child and the worker has difficulty to work with everyone that is why it is important for the everybody to work consistently with a child parents included also.

# Sitting In silence

On this particular day i came on duty and I saw Joan (15 years old) a young girl that i do not have a very strong relationship with at the centre was  sitting and crying in the front of the centre all alone. Remembering that she had a panel meeting earlier today I greeted her and went in to clock in and told the staff on duty that Joan was sitting alone in front of the centre with no adult around. They explained that the panel didn't go as well as we thought it would and her father didn't show up as he promised her the day before he would, and she was looking forward to spending time with him as she missed him very much. and the panel was to discuss her holiday placement for the holidays. They said they have tried to speak to her but she didn't respond to any of them she just ignored them. So i ask her Child and youth care worker that if it's ok for me to take a chance maybe I can get through to her, and she agreed. I walk to the front of the centre to where she is sitting

and sat beside but not to close as to invade her space, and at that moment  my phone ring and i answered it by saying I cannot speak now, So we both looked at each other not saying a word and we continue to sit in silence no one saying a word. After a while Joan got up gave me a hug and smiled and walked on and went inside to the centre.And after that we had a better stronger relationship
She is now  living by her aunt, but before she left I asked her about the wat was her most memorable day she had at the centre and this is what she said
" Mr mo do you remember that day i was crying after my panel meeting and you came to sit next to me and both of us sat there in silence and u didnt ask me what is wrong and you didn't even answer your phone not that moment meant the world to me, because all i needed was someone to be there for me someone just to support me and not push me to speak that was the most memorable moment i had"

What i have learned from this experience is that sometimes we as adults we think we know what kids want and need but we do not. kids are in control of their own lives and they are the authors of their own stories we as adults must sometimes just sit and listen to what they really have to say, or just be a silent supporter.

If i did ask her what was wrong who knows
what answered I would have received from her.
We are still in contact via social media where she
would greet and ask advice or just chat about
everyday things.

Disengagement

This is a period where child and youth care worker prepared a child in care to exit the program to be reunited back to the community or family, depending on how circumstances is at home we either send a child to an independent living program where he/she will live independently and study or work.
During this time the child normally feels overwhelmed with emotions fears of the unknown but also excited about the thought of leaving care and living independently. When exciting it normally happens when a child reach 18 years old or circumstances at home has change for the better, adoption by someone in the community.

## My experience

At Heatherdale children's home we had some
disengagement with children and we followed a
process of children leaving care.
Our aim for this program was to build resilience
in the child and make the child more
independent and self dependent, and the
necessary tools and skills to live independently

How did we achieve this we introduce them to
the mamelani program and they took part in the
proceed program where they learn skills and
independent living.
Then in the last three months we send the child
home on every weekend and we write out the
weekend out report to get information on what
is going on at home.

We with the help of external program look for a school in the area where the child where the child will be living. We check for any youth developmental programs in the community in which the child can participate in, or any counciling where he can attend that is needed for him.
The child still participate in the mamelani proceed program.
Then we exchange contact numbers to keep in contact with the child in the sense of not being a crutch but just be a means of support to the child.

On the day where the child finally leave the Centre we host a party with all the Child and youth care workers and staff, children together. we play a slideshow of all moments that the child has at the centre such as achievements, Outings, Events and times spent with other kids. the moment is normally a tearful event but it's part of the job. The emotions is normally high when we all say our goodbyes and child exchange numbers with other children and staff members at the centre.

we still keep contact with the child just to do check up on progress on how things are going and how child is coping with home environment. We buy the new school clothes for the child and stationary that the child will need to attend the new school and sort out the school fees for the year so the parents can work out a budget for them for having their child back at home .

# OTHER READ ABOUTS

Child And Youth Care information that assisted
me in becoming a successful worker in the
children's home

# "Rapport and relationships: The basis of child care"

## Michael Burns

*ABSTRACT: The smallest or the most basic aspects of child care are often overlooked or underestimated. The manner in which child care workers can approach each child as a separate and unique human being is a critical aspect of professional and humane practices. In relationships, understanding and rapport are based upon particular styles of perceiving the world. This paper presents to the child care worker a background of information useful in developing basic rapport and solid relations with children. It contains case presentations, highlighting the effective strategies and the common mistakes of care givers.*

## Introduction

Perhaps the most important technique for any care giver to master is the ability to develop a good sense of rapport with the child. Many of the strategies employed by workers in the field of child care are employed unconsciously. This article will attempt to make available, through identification and discussion, those strategies that have been developed and time tested.

Rapport is the name given to the magic that emerges when two people interact to form positive or primarily positive impressions or attitudes toward one another. It is a feeling of sameness and accord threaded with a sense of basic trust. Rapport, that first feeling of trust and respect must be present before even the most basic positive relationship is formed. Once rapport is established, it continues to ebb and flow depending on the way the relationship is interpreted by the people within that relationship. Rapport appears to be the core around which all relationships are formed. The more solid and emotionally healthy the core, the more comfortable and growth producing the relationship.

Preparations

At the very base of the ability to form meaningful relationships lies a great deal of self-awareness on the part of the caregiver. A sound knowledge of strengths and weaknesses as well as an awareness of personal patterns and strategies used in relationship building is extremely helpful in avoiding and working through roadblocks that hamper effective rapport building. Attitudes toward helping and the need to help children must be explored to ensure that a healthy focus is maintained in the best interests of the child. Effective caregivers maintain an air of genuineness that can only come from a great deal of personal awareness.

As well as having an awareness of yourself, an awareness of children both in groups and as individuals is essential in efficient relationship building. The ability to predict behaviours, understand group process and respond to physical and emotional development in children, makes the task of building trust and comfort into a relationship much easier. So often care givers, in settings where emotionally disturbed children are the normal population, lose track of normal or average growth and development in children. They often overreact or fail to react to the child's maturational process. Along with this comes the focus on negative areas in the child's life — the problem list.

This focus can taint or cloud other areas or behaviours that may be normal reactions to stimuli provided by the care giver or the treatment setting. Take the example of a seven-year-old child admitted to a treatment setting. The child has just turned seven and has a number of fears on his problem list. Much effort is put in listing these numerous fears and their possible origins. A study of children done by the Gessel Institute shows that children between the ages of six and seven normally experience a great many fears (hg, Ames, 1955). If this seven-year-old child is a *visual* learner it may appear that his fears have become more intense over the past year, causing considerable concern for parents and care givers. A further look into the Gessel study will reveal that the fears of a seven-year-old child are predominantly visual in nature while at six they are predominantly *auditory* (Ilg, Ames, 1955). These circumstances could very well be the reason for the increase in the magnitude of the child's fear. This new information in turn might convince the caregiver to focus treatment on acknowledging the fears and moving toward making this child more comfortable with them. The majority of fears will disappear at or around ages eight and nine (Ilg, Ames, 1955).

In developing rapport and strengthening relationships with children it is most beneficial to have an awareness of the normal growth and development of the cognitive and emotional areas of the child. A general knowledge of these developmental areas of the child can be of much use in understanding and predicting behaviour. Always keep in mind that no one individual child follows perfectly any of the developmental stages presently known to the psychological world (Mussen, Conger, Kagan, 1969). The way the child progresses through stages of development and the way in which he or she expresses the common patterns of behavioural, emotional and cognitive stages vary according to his or her own basic individuality and situation (Ilg, Ames, 1955). When individual differences are considered, however, understanding these levels can serve to assist caregivers in drawing closer to the children in their care.

Sensory modalities

An awareness of sensory modalities can also be useful when attempting to keep in step with children. Human beings tend to have a favourite or preferred sensory modality. This preferred modality can be identified in a number of ways and by various techniques (Dilts *et al*, 1980). Children display characteristics that also make this preferred sensory modality identifiable (Barbe, 1973).

*Visual children*, that is children who organize their world by means of what they see and what they perceive visually, tend to speak using predominantly visual words (Bandler, Grinder, 1976), e.g., "Look, you can *see* the sailboats really clear now dad. *Notice* all the coloured *angles* near the bow. What a *sight*!". These children are often more concerned with their appearance. They also tend to do better in mathematics, as opposed to reading and spelling, in school. Visual children often breath more in the upper cavity of their lungs (Dilts *et al*, 1980). Visual imagery is often more easily attainable for these children and they frequently have vivid and colourful dreams. A visual child often needs to see something before he or she believes it to be true and, therefore, understands best when shown how to accomplish particular tasks. Visual children may tend to look at the person who is speaking more often than others (Barbe, 1973).

*Auditory children*, on the other hand, will speak using words that predominantly relate to sound (Bandler and Grinder, 1976), e.g., "It *sounds* to me like she won't *listen* to what you're *saying* to her. I think she has *turned you off*. These children are real "talkers" and tend to speak early in their development. Their voice tone is apt to give indications of their moods. Their tempo when speaking is often very rhythmic. An auditory child breaths from the diaphragm and usually at a more even rate (Dilts *et al.*, 1980). Reading and spelling are often favourite subjects in school and auditory children may do poorly in math. Auditory children learn best when given verbal instructions and can often listen very well when they appear to be unattentive (Barbe, 1973).

A *kinesthetic child* is someone who learns best through his or her sense of touch and emotions. They speak most often in feeling words (Bandler, Grinder 1976). e.g., "I have a *feeling* that if he does not *get in touch* with what's *bugging* him we are all in for a *rough* time". These children may be labelled "clingers" or "huggers" due to their strong need for physical contact. They are often considered "sloppy", since they pay more attention to how their clothes feel than how they look. These children often breath deep in their abdomens (Dilts *et al.*, 1980). Their voice pitch is slightly lower than visual and auditory children. A kinesthetic child is often the child who is labelled "emotional". They use a lot of hand gestures when speaking and often count on their fingers (Barbe, 1973). These children do well in projects that require making things with their hands. Kinesthetic children usually enjoy crafts and body contact sports.

The above profiles of visual, auditory and kinesthetic children are not "fool proof" and, like developmental stages, we must be aware of the child*s individuality. However, children presenting profiles similar to the ones outlined above can be hypothesized as being either visual, auditory or kinesthetic. Awareness of the common and normal developments of children as well as an appreciation for how they interpret their worlds, adds a new dimension, a clearer perspective on the child care worker*s interpretation of the child*s world and how to relate to it.

Common mistakes and alternate strategies

I believe that human beings tend to grow and learn as much, if not more, from their mistakes, as they do from their successes. Listed below are a series of case examples which will act as representations for some of the more common blunders made in attempting to establish rapport.

Case Study #1

Billy, a twelve-year-old child, was admitted to the residential unit of a children*s mental health centre when the parents were unable to handle his behaviour. He was referred to the centre by the courts following three convictions for minor offenses.

Billy was assigned to Don, a child care worker. Don's first job was to develop some type of rapport with Billy. Billy was acting very aloof with all the staff and tended to interact more with his peers. Don tried everything to establish a positive relationship with Billy, however, he tended to remain "cool" toward Don.

Weeks passed and Billy maintained his casual relationship with Don despite Don's best efforts, until one Monday night, Don happened to catch Billy trying to sneak out of the cottage. Don confronted Billy on his actions, but Billy refused to speak. Don sensed this as being a good opportunity to win the youngster's confidence. He told Billy that he would not report him this time and did, in fact, withhold this information in the hope of establishing a higher level of trust.

Following this event, Billy seemed to get closer to Don. He asked for favours, which Don gave in hopes of building a positive relationship. Billy was fond of playing basketball and Don stretched the rules a little to give Billy more time in the gym. Don also found himself defending Billy when the cottage staff found fault with him.

Their relationship progressed, however, Don's treatment interventions did not. In time, Don felt he had been take advantage of.  Billy felt poorly about himself for manipulating Don. Billy's negative view of himself and his manipulative behaviour was reinforced by Don's ineffective rapport building strategy.

Analysis

Giving special privileges as a way of establishing rapport can be a very ineffective way to build a relationship. Also, some of Don's favours were breaking the policy and rules of the agency. It might appear to Billy that Don has little regard for rules and authority. A consistent and honest approach with children is most important. Their need for time and space should be respected. However, they should not be allowed to manipulate and the same rules should apply to all.

Case Study #2

Sally, an eight-year-old child had been referred for assessment to a hospital out-patient clinic. Jan the psychometrist, met Sally in the playroom and established a base rapport with her by playing house in the waiting room. When they entered the testing room, however, Sally became somewhat withdrawn. Jan assured Sally that everything was okay. Sally responded and began relating positively to Jan again. A short time into the test situation, Sally became resistant to answering Jan's questions. Jan felt it was crucial that Sally answer. She wanted to break Sally's manipulative behaviour by not giving in to her and insisted that she answer. Jan felt that she had a solid bond with Sally and believed that she would respond. Sally did not respond to Jan's questions and refused to speak altogether. Jan tried several times to regain her rapport with Sally but without apparent success.

Analysis

In situations where a child and adult meet for the first time and the child is asked to trust as well as perform, the child needs to have every consideration. The rapport at these initial contacts is very fragile. Children should not be coaxed or tricked into answering questions they are uncomfortable with. Total respect for the child and his or her feelings is most important at these times. In this example, Jan could have put more play activities into the test situation which would have relieved the anxiety around the test. Sometimes completing half a battery of tests with the more sensitive and anxious children is a more productive way to move. Some children do need to be persuaded at times and perhaps Jan's feelings around being "manipulated" were valid. In that case Jan might have left the question unanswered or returned to it at a different time.

Case Study #3

Hank, a very aggressive and "street wise" twelve year old was admitted to a group home. He was referred because of truancy and aggressive behaviour. Some of his aggressive outbursts resulted in assaults and property being destroyed. Hank appeared to have a very negative view of the world. Keith, his assigned worker, implemented a treatment plan designed to change Hank's negative image of himself, and the people with whom he interacted. Keith decided to model a positive image and to minimize most of Hank's negative statements and attitudes. Hank was resistant to this approach and seemed determined to prove Keith wrong by presenting himself as having a negative view of the world. They both ended up in a power struggle which cost Keith whatever rapport he had with Hank.

Analysis

Often children with negative attitudes toward themselves and the world need to be listened to and even encouraged to express such feelings. Aggressive outlets can be introduced to allow the child to express his dislike in an active way. However unsatisfactory such perceptions appear to others, they cannot simply be ignored or invalidated. To approach the problem in this way is to ignore and invalidate the individual. When you discount a negative child on his aggression, chances are you may be discounted in return. Keith's initial approach with Hank was most acceptable. Once this strategy proved ineffective, Keith might have introduced Hank to his negative side and perhaps this could evolve into a "bitch session". Keith might want to give Hank twenty minutes a day where he can be as negative as he wishes (within obvious safety rules) while providing ample opportunity for the development of alternative and more positive attitudes.

Case Study #4

Joanne, a very introverted six-year-old child, was referred to a day care program because of peer difficulties and low self-esteem. Connie, her case worker, was very cautious with Joanne and presented herself as a warm and caring person. Joanne responded to Connie's manner and was making steady progress in their relationship. In the hope of strengthening this relationship, Connie promised Joanne a trip to her apartment which was to include Joanne's first subway ride. Connie had shared with Joanne that she looked a lot like Joanne when she was her age and promised Joanne a look through her photo album. The day came for the trip to Connie's apartment and Joanne was excited. Unfortunately Connie was late picking Joanne up being detained with another child who had an upset. When they finally drove to the apartment Connie had completely forgotten the subway ride. Later, when Connie realized her mistake it did not appear to bother Joanne who was enjoying exploring the apartment. The time went by quickly and soon it was time to take Joanne back. This meant there was no time to look through Connie's photo album, but again this did not appear to disturb Joanne. Joanne returned to the cottage and seemed a little subdued, but it was interpreted as her being fatigued after the long day. Although it appeared that the day had gone well it was noted that Joanne began to systematically distance herself from Connie following the visit. Over time, even the positive ingredients of the initial relationship disappeared.

Analysis

Promises made during the initial rapport building stage can be very dangerous unless great care is taken in their fulfillment. One broken promise can trigger a whole series of memories of broken promises from the past, and promises are usually unnecessary in most cases. A relationship needs to be solid before it can withstand a broken promise. Connie might have planned all these excellent rapport building tactics and not told Joanne. The surprise element would have been greater and this may have eliminated many disappointments.

Techniques for establishing rapport

*1. Reflecting*

Reflecting is a form of "pacing" (Bandler, Grinder, 1975) or "mirroring" and is literally imitating or miming the child's behaviour. The phrase "walking in someone else's shoes" fits comfortably here. This technique is probably the most effective way of establishing quick rapport and is the one, used either consciously or unconsciously, by most care givers and therapists.

A typical strategy for reflecting would proceed as follows:

a. The care giver observes the child being aware of the child's posture and facial expression.

b. The care giver recreates or imitates the child's posture and expression.

c. As the child moves changing posture and expression so the care giver follows mirroring the child. As this mirroring is taking place the care giver is aware of any emotions or physical sensations (e.g., feeling of anger, muscle tension) that he experiences while reflecting the child.

d. Having successfully mirrored the child's posture and expression the care giver begins to use similar word phrases as the child. He or she matches the child's predicates by responding with visual words when the child uses visual predicates, auditory words when the child uses auditory language and similarly with kinesthetic olfactory and questatory language.

e. When the care giver has successfully mirrored and feels comfortable with mirroring the child's language he or she observes some of the child's more subtle behaviours, e.g., breathing depth and rate, gestures and mannerisms, eye and head movements, etc).

f. The care giver then mirrors one or more of these more subtle behaviours.

g. As the child changes these behaviours so the care giver follows by matching them with his or her own behaviours. As in step c. the care giver becomes aware of emotions and physical sensations taking place in his or her body as he or she mirrors the child.

h. Having successfully mirrored the more subtle non-verbal behaviours the care giver now mirrors the more subtle verbal behaviours, e.g., voice tone and tempo, inflections, pronunciations, etc.

i. The care giver's next step is to respond verbally at an emotional level by feeding back verbally the child's feelings both those stated by the child and by questioning those implied by his or her verbal and non-verbal communication.

These steps may be repeated several times during an interaction with a child. It's important not to mimic the child in an obvious way which might make the child feel conscious or agitated. It is a more subtle and unintrusive style that is most effective here.

## 2. *Language*

What we say, how we say it, where we say it, when we say it and why we say it can cause a wide variety of responses from whom we say it to.

Incongruent language, when our words do not match what our body is saying, as well as mixed messages, responding inconsistently to behaviour or even (e.g., laughing when a child throws his food one time and scolding the same child when he throws his food on another occasion) cause the children a great deal of confusion and anxiety. When wishing to develop rapport the care giver is best advised to stay away from these two forms of communication. Congruent and clearly understood language is most helpful when communicating with children. Communication patterns that are non-threatening and non-directive will most often produce honest and genuine responses. Speaking positively and optimistically can help to lighten a child*s mood or help him or her to relax and speak more freely. Humour is an excellent technique to help the child to become more relaxed and feel less threatened. Verbal strokes such as praise, encouragement, compliments or calling the child by his or her first name in many cases have a positive effect on the relationship.

Language and its wide variety of uses can assist the care giver to develop rapport in many constructive and interesting ways.

*3. Physical contact*

Just as we communicate through language so do we speak with our bodies. Touch or physical contact with someone can be a rewarding and meaningful experience. A hand on the shoulder, a pat on the back or a handshake can all communicate acceptance, approval, comfort or welcome. A hug, a back rub, a kiss, holding hands, or an arm around the shoulder, when done appropriately, communicate positive and caring feelings. Physical contact may possibly be the most meaningful method of communicating feelings of acceptance and caring. Children, with very few exceptions, have almost a hunger to be held or touched in some way. Children under stress, either physical, emotional or both, seem to require more physical contact than they might normally require.

Most children have no objection to being touched; however, some children do not like to be touched initially. In most cases it is advisable to ask permission before you touch a child who seems apprehensive around physical contact. There is an invisible boundary or area around all of us called our personal space. This space is different for all of us and most humans are only comfortable allowing certain people into this space. This space should be respected for children at all times being careful not to invade this space until permission is given. Physical contact should be monitored by the care giver in terms of how the child is reacting to being touched. Also, some cultures, families, groups and individuals enjoy being touched more than others; care must be taken not to over-or understimulate these children in a tactile sense. A good strategy here seems to be to make physical contacts with a child only occasionally at first and by monitoring this contact, it can be increased as the relationship develops. Touch is a very powerful, yet very personal way of building trust.

The therapeutic relationship between the child and the care giver, like the mustard seed, can grow into the largest of trees giving protection and shelter for the birds of the air and the animals afoot.

Conclusion

It can be argued that rapport is the most important individual characteristic in assisting children to change and realize their potentials. This skill of developing rapport only comes naturally to those who have had excellent role models, and even then most of these people are not fully aware of what they do to establish rapport. 'Understanding' in any relationship requires that individuals appreciate and respect the way in which the other person perceives himself and the world in general. Rapport and relationship building skills can be taught and practiced and perfected. It is my hope that the awarenesses, techniques and strategies posed in this paper will motivate you to practice and perfect your rapport building skills to help you reach and motivate the children and young adults in your care.

References

Ames, Louis and Ilg, Francis. *The Gesell Institute's Child Behaviour from Birth to Ten.* New York: Harper and Row Publishers, 1955.

Bandler, Richard and Grinder, John. *The Structure of Magic II*. Palo Alto, California: Science and Behaviour Books Inc., 1976.

Barbe, Walter B. What We Know About Modality — A Lecture Given to the 25th Council for Exceptional Children, 1982.

Conger, John, Kagan, Jerome and Mussen, Paul. *Child Development and Personality*. New York: Harper and Row Publishers, 1969.

Dilts, Robert; Grinder, John; Bandler, Richard; Badler, Leslie; and DeLozier, Judith. *Neuro Linguistic Programming, Volume 1. Cupertino, California: Meta Publications, 1980.*

Acknowledgements: *The Journal of Child and Youth Care, Volume 2 Number 2*

Exploiting daily events to heal the
pain of sexual abuse

Lorraine E. Fox

*Abstract: Research and clinical experience indicate that the effects of sexual abuse can be both profound and long-term, sometimes affecting the quality of life for the victim/survivor forever. While the therapeutic benefits of traditional clinical interventions are well documented, it is important that direct caregivers also recognize that they have much to offer child victims in terms of supportive and healing relationships and interventions. Using the Redl model of life-space interventions, the author details specific areas of trauma that can be positively influenced by conscious, intentional, therapeutic day- to-day interactions and interventions by adults in the child/youth's immediate environment. These potential healing agents include child care workers, support staff foster parents, school personnel, volunteers, and family members.*

There are a variety of interventions by a variety of people in different helping positions that can be effective in providing comfort, soothing, new learning and eventual healing for the wounds of abuse. Therapists, direct service child care workers, recreational workers, foster parents, cooks, maintenance personnel, and volunteers each have something significant to contribute to the successful adaptation to life for hurt and hurting children and youth. No contribution is to be seen as "better" or more useful. Working as a team committed to the growth and healing of our wounded young people, we strive together to fill the gaps of love and care, and to teach coping skills that enable a successful and fulfilling life.

Fritz Redl, a pioneer in the elevation of para-professional roles to that of critical importance in the therapeutic life of children, initially coined the notion of "exploiting daily life events" for the restoration of wholeness to fractured, fragmented and vulnerable youngsters (Garfat, 1987; Redl, 1966; Redl & Wineman, 1952). Professional child care literature reveals a strong commitment to utilize the daily routines of group living, such as meals and food (Rose, 1988), chores (Editorial Board, 1992), bedtimes (Augustin, 1984), and the like. We would like to explore specific events and interactions that may occur during the course of a day that can be "exploited" for healing purposes in the lives of sexually traumatized children and youth. First, let us briefly review some of the traumatic aspects of sexual abuse that have the potential to cause distortion and deep wounds, and that pose a risk to successful adjustment. Traumatic sex

Sexual abuse, of course, involves sex. It is a very specific form of abuse with very specific implications. The discomfort of many with the very nature of this form of abuse is conveyed by the common substitution of non-sexual words, such as "molest," to describe it. It is abuse, of course, because it is sex that is unwanted, non-mutual (forceful or coercive), and something for which young children are not physically, mentally, or emotionally prepared. The result of this aspect of the abuse is often referred to as "traumatic sexualization." Workers with sexually abused children/youth should never be surprised or dismayed when part of the abuse trauma is acted out sexually. We know that when children are victimized by violence, there is a tendency to re-enact the violent situation in an attempt to master an event over which they were powerless (Cameron, 1994). Victims of school-yard shootings can be predicted to play "gunman" for a while after the event. And, of course, they insist that they take turns being the gunman.

Using this knowledge, it can be reasonably predicted that victims of terrifying sexual abuse will attempt to gain mastery by engaging in various sexual behaviours and activities. It is not "treatment" to punish such activity. The therapeutic response will be to "exploit" such events to help with the working out, the mastery.

An additional sexual trauma results from the very way kids are "set up" for abuse. Adults do not begin to molest by grabbing a child's genitals, but by offering initial physical contact that is experienced as affection. Before turning sexual, the contact consists of benign touch: sitting on someone's lap, having your back rubbed, snuggling, an arm around the shoulder, or a pat on the thigh. As this contact graduates to sexual intrusiveness, the child becomes confused and is often not even clear about when things changed from "OK" to "not-OK." This confusion is often manifest in touching interactions between abused children/youth and adults who engage with them. How many workers have had a child hug them in a way that felt uncomfortable? How often has a child kissed us on the lips rather than the cheek? Sometimes we have become gradually uneasy as a benign touch from a child turned to touch that had sexual tones. Confusion between sex and affection also results in a variety of symptomatic interactions between child and child, where innocent play turns to sex play, or age-appropriate play promotes sudden rage as memories are triggered. Responses from adults to these events have potential either for further confusion as a result of a harsh response, or for re-education in an area where faulty notions have been formed.

A traumatic component of all abuse is the "powerlessness" experienced by the child, as he or she experiences his or her complete inability to influence the behavior of the hurting adult(s).[1] There is now an abundance of research and longitudinal study that illuminates the life-long effect of such experiences. When powerlessness is introjected, made part of the belief system and adaptation of an individual, we have the frightening phenomenon of "learned helplessness" (Seligman, 1973, 1975). When there is a compensatory reaction to this powerlessness, we find the equally frightening adaptation where the young person begins confusing "power" with "control," and we find the victim now the victimizer; the hurt, now the hurting; the scared now the scary (Groth, 1979; Hunter, 1990).

Betrayal

To be sexually abused is to be betrayed; and to be betrayed is to forever be unsure of who can be trusted. Average children are taught by their parents to fear strangers: don't open the door if you don't recognize the person; don't get into a car if the person is a stranger. Things become clear: if I know you, you're safe; if I don't, I become afraid. Young, and even older, children have a natural recoiling response when meeting new people; hanging onto daddy's hand, hiding behind mom's skirt, backing up and giving clear evidence of wanting out even when being perfectly polite in the greeting. But what if the person who hurt you is someone you were close to? What do you learn about safety if you, in the past, allowed yourself to relax with someone who was nice to you, who offered you friendship and affection, and then gave you sex and terror? Who's to be trusted now? It is crucial that direct service caretakers learn to both expect and understand what may seem like a rejection from a child or adolescent, just when "things seemed to be going so well."

A youngster may run away, ask for a new worker, or just turn strange. This will most likely stem from a deep terror of trusting, based on past experience. The young person will need patience, a stance of acceptance, and an "open arms" policy, allowing them to react to the terror, and then come back to learn that this relationship will not exploit their trust. Too often we find individuals and programs closing the door on those who seem to reject us, rather than making the commitment to hang in with them. Not only is this sad, but terribly unfair.

Secrecy

To be sexually abused is to be incredibly lonely. It is impossible to believe that this could be happening to anyone else. You are told not only not to tell, but that awful things will happen to you if you do tell. You gradually learn to feel "safe" when you are being deceitful; telling the truth will cause terrible things to happen to you or your family, and your molester, about whom you are usually very ambivalent. (While not usually ambivalent about wanting the sex to stop, many children are quite ambivalent about their feelings toward the person who is abusing them.) Better to be quiet, or to lie. Truth begins to equal danger. You develop a habit pattern of saying little: "OK," "not much," "nothing." Or you learn to use sounds instead of words, grunting in response to questions, using gestures. Perhaps you learn to employ "empty speech": lots of words with no substance or meaning, which sounds like you're sharing, but you're not really saying anything. Or, you just learn to lie: Say you had fun; lie about where you went, why you were late, what you did. Whatever you do, don't give it away. You become very adept at covering up what's happening. "Good boy/girl," says the molester. "Good girl/boy," implies the parent of the child who really doesn't want to know. Over what period of time was the child/youth in your care sexually molested? A year, two years, more? Count the days. Three years of keeping a secret equals more than a thousand days of practice in deception. A thousand days of profound loneliness. The secret becomes as painful as the sex. How cruel to "punish" kids for lying, when that is the only safety they've known until now.

There was a recent incident in a residential treatment centre in the author's state where a resident successfully committed suicide in the facility by hanging himself. While investigating the death, it was learned that while the young person did not share his intention with any adult staff, he did, in fact, confide in a number of his peers. Not one child said a word, until it was too late. Why? Not for any malicious reasons, but because collections of abused children/youth are, unfortunately, entirely comfortable with secrets, and very fearful of the consequences of truth. How urgent that we keep this in mind while attempting to provide safety for our vulnerable residents.

Lack of protection

It takes more than an "offender" for a child to be abused. Perhaps we have become overly focused on those who overtly hurt our children. If we can step into the experience of an abused child, we realize that abuse requires more than someone hurting you; it also requires a non-protector. No one can hurt you if someone protects you. When you lie or stand there, feeling or being forced to let someone touch you, being forced to touch sexual parts of an adult, bleeding from being penetrated, gagging from feeling suffocated, you wonder not only why someone is doing this to you, but why someone isn't stopping it! How can they go on pretending it's not happening? Why can't they see behind my feeble lies? Why can't they see and feel my pain and fear?

There are more traumatic components to sexual abuse, but let's focus on how events in the daily "life-space" present opportunities to be helpful with these.

Traumatic sexualization

There are a myriad of daily activities that can prompt a symptomatic response to real or perceived sexual stimuli for sexually abused children/youth: Sharing a bathroom, showering/bathing, dressing, gym class, contact playing, adult affection, bedtime. Let's hone our observation skills to see and hear what our youngsters are telling us (usually with behaviour rather than words). Do we need to be more sensitive with regard to providing privacy for children for bathroom activities? Can we "read" the unnecessary layers of clothing as a signal that the young person does not feel safe, and does not feel able to protect him or herself without clothing used as armor? Can we give them comfort and reassurance at night: a night-light, a roommate, some music to listen to while falling asleep, awake staff, permission to sleep in clothes if too scared to put on pajamas?

Are we *talking* about sex? Sexually abused children have trouble with sex! We are now able to correct their distortions and misinformation. We can give them education and re-education. Are there books to read? Are they accessible? Do we have regular conversations about sex and how it is supposed to be, and about how hard it is to have it introduced into young lives before nature intended? When sexual remarks are made at the dinner table, do we hush the child(ren), or do we postpone the discussion until after dinner, but schedule a time to talk about what was brought up? Have staff told kids explicitly that they are open to questions about sex? We want to monitor our responses to their sexual behaviour (talk or activity) to be sure we are not causing shame about something the child had no control over. Sexual talk, and sexual activity, provide wonderful opportunities for us to interact with kids about a part of their life that they cannot deal with alone. They have questions and wonder if anyone has answers.

Of course we don't always have good answers, but we can always be clear that we are not hiding anything from them, leaving them to imagine what might have happened to them. We don't want to leave our immature young minds on their own to figure out what's happened to them: and if we don't help, they will. The author can assure you that there is an inverse relationship between sexual activity and verbalization: the less adults are willing to talk, the more kids will sort out and act out their concerns behaviourally.[2]

Staff and other helping adults are in a wonderful position to use their own experiences and interactions with youth to help them gain insight and sort through their confusion. We can use uncomfortable touch to teach exactly what makes it uncomfortable, and why, and to provide guidance about more acceptable physical interaction. We can use activity between peers to try to understand the *meaning* of the activity for the children. If we can find out what they were trying to understand or solve with the sexual interaction, we can help them do so more appropriately... with us. Staff can use displays of affection between them, which invariably produce hoots of innuendo, to discuss differences between sexual and affectionate touch. (This, of course, implies that we have done work on the treatment team to ensure that they have developed positive enough feelings between the members that displays of affection — back rubs, hugs, and so on — are likely!)

Another very challenging aspect of interventions with sexual behaviour is the opportunity to join the struggle experienced by same-sex abused youth. In my work with organizations, I have found this probably the most "loaded" issue for staff to deal with. Literature on sexual abuse reveals that, as far as we know from reported cases, offenders are more often men, whether the child-victim is male or female. This presents specific trauma for male victims abused by men, since many questions and fears arise with regard to the effects of same-sex abuse on sexual development. Specifically, boys (usually) must resolve two very complex—and controversial— issues: resolving their sexual identity as well as their sexual orientation. It is important to distinguish between these two processes, because they are quite separate, although many cultural stereotypes cause them to seem fused. (Gay men do not, because they are gay, feel and act like women. Lesbians do not, because they are gay, feel and act like men.)

*Sexual identity* has to do with one's comfort and acceptance with one's maleness or femaleness. Because of many cultural roles, some boys see victimization as a "girl" problem, and thus have difficulty living with their former inability to control abusive situations, especially sexual ones, which are often not overtly forceful. This discomfort sometimes causes post-pubertal and adolescent boys to become estranged and alienated from their vulnerable small-boy past, and to thus risk losing "empathy" for others who are hurt. Adults can be very helpful in re-framing the abuse as a crime of adults against children, which is not sex-specific. We can also try to keep them in touch with the realistic reasons for their compliance: smallness in size, vulnerability to the relationship, and conformity to the expectation of obedience. A very simple, practical intervention with some boys is to simply take them to a school or play yard and show them small boys — to give permission, as it were, for their past behaviour.

It is crucial that our male victims not lose touch with their vulnerable self, for an unfortunate characteristic of many abusers is lack of "empathy" for their victims, which stems from lack of empathy for themselves.

*Sexual orientation* is a separate developmental process, and has to do with the development of an emotional and sexual feeling for one's own sex. In our "homophobic" society this can lead to an incredibly lonely, and sometimes dangerous, journey for teens as they try to understand themselves. Perhaps a teen girl's only experience with intercourse was during the abuse, which she hated; she then might wonder if she doesn't like men. Perhaps a young boy had some sexual pleasure during the abuse, although the context was miserable, leading him to wonder if he's gay. Some same-sex molested youth come to believe that they've been "made" a homosexual by the abuser. The rate of suicide for gay youth is frightening; and suicide is a result of loneliness and hopelessness. We owe our abused youth relationships in which they can sort out their questions and feelings without recrimination and condemnation.

Feelings of powerlessness

We can study the daily behaviour of children in our care to see how they are struggling with their anger about having been powerless to influence adult behaviour. Are they showing us that they are becoming comfortable (i.e., used to) being victims. Do they turn to others to solve their problems? Are they allowing themselves to be scapegoated? Who are they dating and how do they allow themselves to be treated? Are they, rather, showing us that they are reacting to their victimization by identifying with the aggressor, believing that it is better to "give it" than to "get it"? Are they beginning to feel "powerful" when they are controlling others?

It is not helpful for staff to solve problems for children/youth, because it reinforces for the child/youth that he or she can't. It is more important that adults teach problem-solving skills; that coaching is provided, not interference. When peers are having trouble with each other, work with them to solve it, but don't solve it for them.

# Working through betrayal

It is important to be alert for signs of "panic" when a young person starts to feel too comfortable. They often "blow" a placement, or a relationship, when they realize they are letting their guard down and relaxing too much. It reminds them of when they did this before, and then got done in! We want to be careful not to reject a child when he or she rejects us. We want to examine our willingness to "hang on" to someone who's too scared to stick with us right now. Can we wait for the runner to return? Can we use care before assigning a new worker? It is important to provide opportunities for betrayed young people to learn that getting close and feeling vulnerable does not always result in being "used" or hurt by someone. When a child/ youth makes an overt sexual gesture, or offers an explicit sexual favour, we can show care to respond not to the language, which is not the issue, but to the "real" question: are you interested in having sex with me? The most reassuring response is the most explicit: not "don't be silly," but "I'm not interested in having sex with children."

We want to look, also, at signs that bewilderment over trust is not causing youngsters to be careless with their personal safety. Many of our young people feel perfectly comfortable getting into a car full of strangers, letting someone they don't know hold them or take them by the hand. Great patience is needed to give good information about personal safety, while not discounting their previous experience.

Learning to live with the truth

The longer a child/young person has had to live fearing the truth, that is, discovery of their "secret," the more patient we must be with their inclination to avoid honesty. It is crucial that we not moralize this behaviour: it has nothing to do with values or morality, it had to do with their very survival, as they understood it. Punishing these children for lying serves to reinforce the notion that the truth is dangerous. Opportunities must be provided for them to try saying scary things out loud, without retribution. Obviously, this complicates interactions in group settings! We don't want to compromise our belief that "honesty is the best policy," but we also can't afford to be naive. Sexually abused children/youth have been taught something quite different. Learning to hear the "sound" of reality can take a very long time. One of our uncomfortable tasks is to examine our own interactions: are they honest? Do staff say out loud what it really is, or do we also compromise truth, rationalizing away our reasons for not confronting each other, for giving children less than complete information.

"Wimps" need not apply

Abused youngsters cannot heal or feel safe when in the care of those overwhelmed with the job! Stress junkies, step right up. The job will never get easy. The challenges never stop. Not everyone with a good heart is suited. Hire, pay, and reward those who actually enjoy the challenges of working with troubled and troubling children. Beware of getting caught in the "bar at closing time" trap when there are staff shortages: remember that people look better to us when we're desperate than they should.

Sexually abused children are either abused by women, or not protected by women, which places a strong burden/opportunity on women to demonstrate protective skills. It is urgent that women not back off in favour of men during explosive situations. Sexually abused children have either been abused by men, or abandoned by men. Strong, nurturing, "present" men can teach new roles. It is crucial that all adults in the environment demonstrate protection skills, or we fail our mission and release young people who will produce children with no notions of how to protect them: by sticking around, by knowing what's going on, by not allowing others to hurt or get hurt, by facing the truth. All of you "clucking mother hens" out there... go for it! What a gift to abused kids. Find out what they're up to. Ask questions. Be nosy. Give and get lots of information. Let's also be sure to have caring male workers who are not just biding time until they can move "up," and away from the kids. Loving and caring for kids is not a "woman thing." Kids are owed—and their future kids are owed—strong and protective men and women to keep them safe now, and to show how it's done.

Reasons for optimism

Each day, in hundreds of ways, those who attempt to "help" those who need us are provided with a multitude of opportunities. We may not know exactly what to say, and it doesn't matter. Kids will know if we have taken the trouble to understand their experience, and this can always be communicated. If we are willing to take a step in their shoes (and those shoes do hurt!), we can walk with them into new ways of looking at the world, new ways of learning to carefully trust, new ways to exercise personal power so they can be in charge of their own safety. What a wonderful way to spend a life!

Notes

1. For a more complete discussion of the effects of, and therapeutic interventions with, the experience of powerlessness for victims, see Fox,1994.

2. Solicited reports from agencies the author has worked with, who reported a sometimes dramatic decrease in covert sexual activity in response to changes in staff openness about sexuality. See also Fox, 1989.

References

Augustin, G. (1984). Late evening rounds in residence. *Journal of Child and Youth Care, 1*(1), 32-33.

Cameron, C. (1994). Veterans of a secret war: Survivors of childhood sexual trauma Compared to Vietnam war veterans with PTSD. *Journal of Interpersonal Violence, 9*(1), 117-132.

Editorial Board. (1992). Who needs chores? *Die Kinderversorger, 10*(6), 7-8.

Fox, L.E. (1989). *Effects of a training program on the responses of direct service care workers to the sexual behavior of children in child care institutions.* Unpublished dissertation.

Fox, L.F. (1994). The catastrophe of compliance. *Journal of Child and Youth Care, 9*(1), 13-21.

Garfat, T. (1987). Words that have meaning: Reflections on the words of Dr. Fritz Redl. *Residential Treatment for Children & Youth, 5*(2), 5-12.

Groth, N. (1979). Sexual trauma in the life histories of rapists and child molesters. *Victimology: An International Journal, 4,* 93-117.

Hunter, M. (1990). *Abused boys: The neglected victims of sexual abuse.* San Francisco: Lexington Books.

Redl, F. (1966). *When we deal with children: Selected writings.* New York: Free Press.

Redl, F., & Wineman, D. (1952). *Controls from within: Techniques for the treatment of the aggressive child.* New York: Free Press.

Rose, M. (1988). The function of food in a residential treatment process. *Residential Treatment for Children & Youth,* 6(1), 43 — 60.

Seligman: M.E.P. (1973). *Fall into hopelessness. Psychology Today,* 7(1), 43-47.

Seligman, M.E.P. (1975). *Helplessness.* San Francisco: Freeman.

This feature: Fox, Lorraine (1995) Exploiting daily events to heal the pain of sexual abuse. *Journal of Child and Youth Care. 10* (2). pp 33-42

# Stages of social-emotional development in children and teenagers

**Erik Erikson**

*An overview of the developmental tasks involved in the social and emotional development of children and teenagers which continues into adulthood. Based on the Eight Stages of Development developed by psychiatrist, Erik Erikson in 1956.*

According to Erikson, the socialization process consists of eight phases — the "eight stages of man." His eight stages of man were formulated, not through experimental work, but through wide-ranging experience in psychotherapy, including extensive experience with children and adolescents from low — as well as upper and middle — social classes. Each stage is regarded by Erikson as a "psychosocial crisis," which arises and demands resolution before the next stage can be satisfactorily negotiated. These stages are conceived in an almost architectural sense: satisfactory learning and resolution of each crisis is necessary if the child is to manage the next and subsequent ones satisfactorily, just as the foundation of a house is essential to the first floor, which in turn must be structurally sound to support and the second story, and so on.

Erikson's eight stages of development

**1.** *Learning Basic Trust Versus Basic Mistrust (Hope)* Chronologically, this is the period of infancy through the first one or two years of life. The child, well-handled, nurtured, and loved, develops trust and security and a basic optimism. Badly handled, he becomes insecure and mistrustful.

**2.** *Learning Autonomy Versus Shame (Will)* The second psychosocial crisis, Erikson believes, occurs during early childhood, probably between about 18 months or 2 years and 3½ to 4 years of age. The "well-parented" child emerges from this stage sure of himself, elated with his new found control, and proud rather than ashamed. Autonomy is not, however, entirely synonymous with assured self-possession, initiative, and independence but, at least for children in the early part of this psychosocial crisis, includes stormy self-will, tantrums, stubbornness, and negativism. For example, one sees may 2 year olds resolutely folding their arms to prevent their mothers from holding their hands as they cross the street. Also, the sound of "NO" rings through the house or the grocery store.

**3.** *Learning Initiative Versus Guilt (Purpose)*
Erikson believes that this third psychosocial
crisis occurs during what he calls the "play
age," or the later preschool years (from about
3½ to, in the United States culture, entry into
formal school). During it, the healthily
developing child learns: (1) to imagine, to
broaden his skills through active play of all
sorts, including fantasy (2) to cooperate with
others (3) to lead as well as to follow.
 Immobilized by guilt, he is: (1) fearful (2)
hangs on the fringes of groups (3) continues to
depend unduly on adults and (4) is restricted
both in the development of play skills and in
imagination.

**4.** *Industry Versus Inferiority (Competence)*
Erikson believes that the fourth psychosocial
crisis is handled, for better or worse, during
what he calls the "school age," presumably up
to and possibly including some of junior high
school. Here the child learns to master the more
formal skills of life: (1) relating with peers
according to rules (2) progressing from free
play to play that may be elaborately structured
by rules and may demand formal teamwork,
such as baseball and (3) mastering social
studies, reading, arithmetic. Homework is a
necessity, and the need for self-discipline
increases yearly. The child who, because of his
successive and successful resolutions of earlier
psychosocial crisis, is trusting, autonomous,
and full of initiative will learn easily enough to
be industrious. However, the mistrusting child
will doubt the future. The shame- and guilt-
filled child will experience defeat and
inferiority.

**5.** *Learning Identity Versus Identity Diffusion (Fidelity)* During the fifth psychosocial crisis (adolescence, from about 13 or 14 to about 20) the child, now an adolescent, learns how to answer satisfactorily and happily the question of "Who am I?" But even the best-adjusted of adolescents experiences some role identity diffusion: most boys and probably most girls experiment with minor delinquency; rebellion flourishes; self-doubts flood the youngster, and so on.

Erikson believes that during successful early adolescence, mature time perspective is developed; the young person acquires self-certainty as opposed to self-consciousness and self-doubt. He comes to experiment with different — usually constructive — roles rather than adopting a "negative identity" (such as delinquency). He actually anticipates achievement, and achieves, rather than being "paralyzed" by feelings of inferiority or by an inadequate time perspective. In later adolescence, clear sexual identity — manhood or womanhood — is established. The adolescent seeks leadership (someone to inspire him), and gradually develops a set of ideals (socially congruent and desirable, in the case of the successful adolescent). Erikson believes that, in our culture, adolescence affords a "psychosocial moratorium," particularly for middle- and upper-class American children. They do not yet have to "play for keeps," but can experiment, trying various roles, and thus hopefully find the one most suitable for them.

6. *Learning Intimacy Versus Isolation (Love)*
The successful young adult, for the first time,
can experience true intimacy — the sort of
intimacy that makes possible good marriage or
a genuine and enduring friendship.

7. *Learning Generativity Versus Self-Absorption
(Care)* In adulthood, the psychosocial crisis
demands generativity, both in the sense of
marriage and parenthood, and in the sense of
working productively and creatively.

8. *Integrity Versus Despair (Wisdom)* If the other seven psychosocial crisis have been successfully resolved, the mature adult develops the peak of adjustment; integrity. He trusts, he is independent and dares the new. He works hard, has found a well-defined role in life, and has developed a self-concept with which he is happy. He can be intimate without strain, guilt, regret, or lack of realism; and he is proud of what he creates-his children, his work, or his hobbies. If one or more of the earlier psychosocial crises have not been resolved, he may view himself and his life with disgust and despair.

These eight stages of man, or the psychosocial crises, are plausible and insightful descriptions of how personality develops but at present they are descriptions only. We possess at best rudimentary and tentative knowledge of just what sort of environment will result, for example, in traits of trust versus distrust, or clear personal identity versus diffusion. Helping the child through the various stages and the positive learning that should accompany them is a complex and difficult task, as any worried parent or teacher knows. Search for the best ways of accomplishing this task accounts for much of the research in the field of child development.

Socialization, then is a learning-teaching process that, when successful, results in the human organism's moving from its infant state of helpless but total egocentricity to its ideal adult state of sensible conformity coupled with independent creativity.

This feature: Public domain article

### Teenage gambling

Terri Rodriguez Ohlms, M.S.W., L.C.S.W., BCD

The Connecticut Clearinghouse, Wheeler Clinic, Inc. funded by Department of Mental Health and Addiction Services (DMHAS) reported that "Kids and teenagers have always gambled, whether at marbles or flipping baseball cards. Some teens wager on sports, lotteries, jai alai matches, horse and dog races, card playing, as well as at bingo, casinos and video gaming machines. Opportunities to gamble are everywhere, and access is increasing. Some students gamble regularly, while as many a 85 percent have tried their hand at some form of gambling."

According to Chris Armentano, Director of Compulsive Gambling Treatment Program of DMHAS, "For some teens gambling becomes a part of their identity. Gambling stimulates a FALSE image of a special, adequate or unique self. This image often stands in contrast to an underlying self image that is unimportant, inadequate and less than ordinary. Nelson Rose suggested that in each school, there are students known as gamblers. He reports that they are the ones who would "rather go to jai alai than go on a date, run football or world series pools, are sought out for gambling information or to place bets. They might be good students, athletes, in the centre of things or on the fringe. They might be outcasts who seek out gambling for escape and to be with other "losers." They may use gambling in combination with alcohol and other drugs to feel good.

Gipta and Derevnsky of Canada claim that today's adolescents are the first to live their entire lives in a society of legalized gambling. Gambling opportunities are available at local corner stores, restaurants and bars. Lotteries, pulltabs, sports betting and casinos have become part of everyday life for many people. Although it remains illegal for minors to gamble on most government-regulated activities, the willingness of gambling operators to turn a blind eye to juvenile gambling, given the large revenues generated, results in children and adolescents becoming very much a part of the industry.

In Missouri, the minimum legal age to place a bet in lottery, pari-mutuel betting, charity bingo and pull-tabs is 18. For casinos and slot machines it is 21. Do you know what the legal age for betting is in your state?

The commonly accepted definition of problem gambling is "a level of gambling that creates problems for the gambler and his/her family." The level of gambling may interfere with personal relationships, school or work and may include diversion of funds needed for other purchases to the gambling activity. Furthermore, the adolescent may incur debts of substantial amounts to continue the activity.

Motives for gambling as reported by adolescents include relaxation, enjoyment, excitement, entertainment, adventure, attention, opportunity and negative feelings. The typical teen gambler is reported likely to come from homes where gambling is a conspicuous activity, successful, motivated, intelligent (with an IQ of 115 to 120+), competitive, with a history of good to excellent school performance, where alcohol/substance abuse has not been regular behavior. The teen may have abandoned hobbies and extracurricular activities, or he/she may be a perfectionist, easily bored in social settings, looking for new situations to keep up feelings and hold high expectations of self and others.

Indicators of problem gambling in teens can be any of the following:

Family Behavior

• withdrawal from the family

• excessive TV sports watching

- increased irritability or hostility

- lying concerning whereabouts

Personal Behavior

- overly excited or upset at games' outcomes

- interest in non-allegiance sports teams

- unusual devotion to sports-results periodicals

- uncharacteristic phone usage

- absence from school or classes

- tardiness to school

- drop in school grades

Money/Valuables

- unexplained need for money

- borrowing money from family and friends

- exaggerated display of money and other possessions

- missing valuables from home

Preferences

• frequent cards/dice games at home

• late night calls

Possessions

• gambling paraphernalia

• 1-900 phone numbers

• phone charges to sports-results scales

• lottery tickets

• IOUs

• betting slips

Severe gambling problems originate during the pre-teen and adolescent years or younger, and parents often serve as role models for gambling. Parents' preferences may also dictate the types of gambling in which teens participate. In fact, teens may be involved in any of the following, according to preferences:

• card playing

- lottery tickets

- bingo sports pool

- electronic gambling devices

- sports lottery tickets

- games of skill

Not surprisingly, most 9–14-year-olds gamble in their homes with their families. Although youth seem to be aware that gambling is primarily driven by luck, they also believe they can exert meaningful amounts of skill while gambling, endorsing the "illusion of control." The most reported reason was for the enjoyment and excitement it provides.

Adolescent pathological and social gamblers have basic differences, stemming from whether the behavior is part of the gambler's integrated activity or rather an all-consuming obsession. For instance, pathological gamblers are more likely to have a parent who gambles excessively, and gambling makes the pathological gambler feel more important than his or her non-pathological peers. Also, pathological gamblers report borrowing money to finance their gambling habits and more engagement in illegal acts such as stealing. Pathological gamblers express a preoccupation with the "when and how" of the next gambling event.

Treatment requires a psychiatric evaluation ruling out biochemical addictions, impulse control disorders, bi-polar disorder, hypomanic disorder, obsessive-compulsive disorder and anti-social personality disorder. There may be need for psychotropic medications such as SSRIs or mood stabilizers.

A cognitive-behavioral counseling strategy focusing on reality therapy is highly recommended along with required abstinence of mood-altering drugs, especially if biochemical addictions are present and attendance at self-help support groups is for a lasting recovery. The teens must be taught the following "Healthy Decision Making Process" and will need to reframe their "illusion of control" beliefs.

Five Steps of Decision Making

1. Identify the Problem.

2. Consider all possible solutions.

3. Consider the consequences for each possible solution.

4. Select one healthy solution and act on it.

5. Evaluate the results of the solution. Will it be selected in the future?

Considering the Consequences of Decision Making

1. Some decisions are easier than others.

2. Some decisions carry more consequences than others.

3. The consequences of some decisions can hurt.

4. Some decisions make you feel good.

5. Sometimes you cannot make decisions alone.

Evaluating a Solution

1. Was this a good solution for everyone?

2. Was this solution worth the resources needed?

3. Was anything learned that can be applied to other problems?

4. Were goals reached, if any?

5. Would this solution be selected again?

The following illusions of control beliefs are growing among adults and are being passed onto our youth. Examine your thinking and see how realistic it is.

Has your belief system also been affected by the "Hustling" (gaming) industry?

- One day I'm going to strike it rich by winning the lottery.
- I think I have the power to will my numbers to come up.
- To win at gambling, one must think positive thoughts.
- If I concentrate hard enough, I can affect the results of the slots.
- I need to win enough money at gambling to balance my budget.
- If I really want to get ahead, I need to win money at gambling.
- Winning is important to me.
- I wouldn't mind losing $100 because I can win it back.
- I can beat the system if I study it enough.
- I need to adopt the right system to win.
- I can beat the casino if I can learn its system.

Dene S.Berman and Jennifer Davis-Berman

Outdoor educators have explored the therapeutic uses of camping, expeditions, and challenge courses since the 1930s. This feature provides a brief historical synopsis of the parallel development of both outdoor education and outdoor therapeutic programs in working with troubled and adjudicated youth. It also describes the rationale supporting the use of outdoor approaches, the findings from a recent study of outdoor therapeutic methods, and the findings from the few research and evaluation studies that have been conducted to measure the effect of these approaches.

## Historical roots

Some of the earliest attempts using the out-of-doors as a healing environment took place in the "tent therapy" programs at state hospitals during the early 1900s (Davis-Berman & Berman, 1994). For a brief period, a number of articles appeared in the psychiatric literature reporting the therapeutic benefits of moving certain psychiatric patients out of the buildings and into tents set up on the lawns of psychiatric hospitals. Although these programs provided anecdotal evidence of benefits for the patients, they were haphazard at best. By 1920, such accounts disappeared from the literature.

In the mid-1900s, more sophisticated camping programs for troubled youth began, some that included observation, diagnosis, and psychotherapy components. The University of Michigan Fresh Air Camp employed trained counselors and staff psychologists to treat campers selected because of their mental health problems. Similarly, the Salesmanship Club Camp (Dallas, Texas) was founded in 1946 to serve emotionally troubled children. Its founder, Campbell Loughmiller, believed therapeutic wilderness programs should include the perception of danger and immediate natural consequences for lack of cooperation on the part of campers. According to Loughmiller, successfully confronting danger built self-esteem, and suffering natural consequences taught the real need for cooperation.

A parallel development of experience-based programming also was taking place in schools and universities, beginning midcentury and continuing on into the 1970s. The two movements had many common influences, including early thinkers such as John Dewey (1938) and Kurt Hahn, an important figure in the international development of the Outward Bound program beginning in the 1940s. Hahn believed that it was essential to develop both the bodies and minds of students. He was also strongly committed to the notion of community and service (James, 1993). These early ideas helped shape Outward Bound as one of the most influential experiential programs operating to this day. The interested reader is referred to Miner and Boldt (1981) and James (1993) for a history of Outward Bound.

From the decade of the 1970s to the present day, there has been growing interest in experiential learning and outdoor programs. The Project Adventure program, bringing experiential methods and techniques into the public school, was founded in 1971. On an international level, the Association for Experiential Education was officially founded in 1977, as was the Wilderness Education Association (contact information for these organizations is listed below).

Since the 1970s, there has been a dramatic increase in the number and types of outdoor programs geared specifically toward troubled youth. Prior to discussing these programs we will briefly review the rationale behind the use of the out-of-doors in working with troubled youth.

Why use the out-of-doors?

There are aspects of traditional program settings that inhibit the emotional growth and education of some individuals. Most change efforts involve verbal interchanges between staff and participant. This is not an effective way of reaching many people, especially adolescents who may be resistant to talking or who lack trust in adult authority figures. Outdoor programs offer a physically active way for staff and participants to relate to one another, so the emphasis is not solely on talk.

Outdoor programs also place troubled youth in unique settings where they are often quite unsure of themselves. Moving out of the usual environment sometimes serves to reduce defensiveness and change relationships with adult leaders. Many programs incorporate an element of perceived risk, thereby encouraging participants to move beyond their comfort zones and face their issues and fears. Finally, many outdoor programs use a small-group format and encourage interdependence among group members. In expedition programs, where participants and leaders venture out into natural settings for extended periods of time, the 24-hour-a-day group experience becomes very powerful.

Varieties of programs

For purposes of this article, we define troubled youth as those who have mental health problems (diagnosed by a psychiatrist and considered in need of counseling) or who are in the juvenile court system. The vast majority of programs for youths fall under these two categories.

*Mental health programs*

Information about mental health programs was solicited in a national survey conducted by Davis-Berman, Berman, and Capone (1994). The results included several major findings:

- programs can be categorized as inpatient, outpatient, residential, or expedition types;
- the majority of all programs are offered by private agencies;
- most inpatient programs are also run by private agencies;
- taken together, the programs deal with a wide range of problems and issues of youth; and

- the most common problems and concerns include behavioral problems, school and family problems, conduct disorders, self-esteem issues, depression, and suicidal ideation.

The extent of the use of the outdoor environment varied among the mental health programs. Some programs, most notably those based in hospitals, use the outdoors primarily through a ropes course experience. Other programs offer backpacking or canoeing programs for youth who live in the surrounding community (they return to their homes after trips). Still others offer more lengthy expeditions. Participants in expedition programs usually reside at a base camp, from which they travel.

The therapeutic approaches reported by these programs are often quite vague. Those programs that focus on substance abuse issues use a 12-step approach. Others mention "metaphor therapy," while some rely on more traditional individual and group therapy approaches in their outdoor settings.

*Court programs*

There are far greater numbers of mental health programs than there are court-related programs for juveniles. However, there is a great deal of overlap between these categories. The majority of court-related programs are residential in nature and long-term in their approach. They are often designed as an alternative to traditional incarceration, and usually involve expeditions led out of a more traditional treatment centre setting. Some programs have juveniles living in a base camp setting year round, augmented by intensive wilderness outings run from the base camp. Other court-related programs use the outdoor environment to a lesser extent. These programs use some of the ropes course experiences or run short wilderness excursions.

Do these programs work?

The effectiveness of outdoor therapeutic programs is a critical issue, particularly when such programs are used as alternatives to either incarceration or hospitalization for troubled youth. A comprehensive discussion of the research in this area is beyond the scope of this brief report. The interested reader is referred to the literature for in-depth review and discussion of research issues (e.g., Davis-Berman & Berman, 1994; Gass, 1993; Miles & Priest, 1990). Generally, the research on outdoor programs has been sparse and has had some methodological difficulties. However, a number of good studies have been done, which have provided evidence of the effectiveness of these programs:

- Studies of mental health programs have shown widely reported increases in self-esteem of participants and a positive impact on self efficacy.

- Evaluation studies on delinquency programs have shown similar positive gains in self-esteem and reductions in recidivism rates compared with participants involved in traditional programs.
- A recent meta-analysis (Cason & Gillis, 1994) of 43 research studies using experiential education techniques with troubled youth found effect sizes in the moderate range.

These studies suggest generally positive results for outdoor programs for troubled teens, but more research needs to be done. Presently most mental health programs are not evaluating their effectiveness and those that do often have methodological problems.

Critical issues and resources

Unanswered questions in this field that would benefit from more study include the following:

- What can adventure education contribute to therapeutic programs?

- For which participants are outdoor approaches most effective?
- To what standards should therapeutic programs be held accountable?
- What should be the qualifications for professional staff in this field?

Yet, enough anecdotal evidence from early programs and evaluation results from recent programs exists to warrant positive statements about the usefulness of outdoor programs in addressing the needs of this complex and challenging group of young people.

References

Cason, D., & Gillis, H. L. (1994). A meta-analysis of outdoor adventure programming with adolescents. *Journal of Experiential Education, 17*(1), 40-47.

Davis-Berman, J., & Berman, D. S. (1994). *Wilderness therapy: Foundations, theory and research.* Dubuque, IA: Kendall/Hunt.

Davis-Berman, J., Berman, D., & Capone, L. (1994). Therapeutic wilderness programs: A national survey. *Journal of Experiential Education, 17*(2), 49-53.

Dewey, J. (1938). *Experience and education.* NY: Collier Books.

Gamson, Z. F. (1989). *Higher education and the real world: The story of CAEL.* Wolfeboro, NH: Longwood Academic.

Gass, M. (Ed.). (1993). *Adventure therapy: Therapeutic applications of adventure programming.* Dubuque, IA: Kendall/Hunt.

James, T. (1993). *The only mountain worth climbing: The search for roots.* Unpublished manuscript. Garrison, NY: Outward Bound.

Miles, J., & Priest, S. (Eds.). (1990). *Adventure Education.* State College, PA: Venture Publishing.

Miner, J., & Boldt, J. (1981). *Outward Bound U.S.A.: Learning through experience in adventure-based education.* NY: William Morrow. (ED 215 811)______

The organizations mentioned in this article:

Association for Experiential Education, 2885 Aurora Avenue, #28, Boulder, CO 80303-2252

Project Adventure, Inc. P.O. Box 100, Hamilton, MA 01936

Wilderness Education Association, Department of Natural Resources, Recreation and Tourism , Colorado State University, Fort Collins, CO 80523

*Dene S. Berman is a practicing psychologist at Lifespan Counseling Associates and clinical professor of professional psychology at Wright State University (Dayton, Ohio). Jennifer Davis-Berman is a social worker, an associate professor in the Department of Sociology, Anthropology and Social Work at the University of Dayton, and a therapist at Lifespan Counseling Associates.*

## Teaching conflict resolution

*Edna C. Olive*

*We should not have to settle all conflict situations in our groups — only those which fall through the cracks of our better programming. What can we learn from schools which implement "better hygiene" principles?*

*Too many of our young people are caught up in conflicts every day that they do not know how to manage teasing, jealousy and physical aggression. Juvenile delinquency and violence are symptoms of youth's inability to manage conflict in their lives. Teaching youth how to manage conflict in a productive way can help reduce incidents of violent behavior. Conflict resolution education is a beneficial component of a comprehensive violence prevention and intervention program in schools and communities.*

*Conflict resolution education encompasses problem solving in which the parties in dispute express their points of view, voice their interests, and find mutually acceptable solutions. Conflict resolution education programs help the parties recognize that while conflict happens all the time, people can learn new skills to deal with conflict in nonviolent ways. The programs that appear to be most effective are comprehensive and involve multiple components such as the problem-solving processes and principles of conflict resolution, the basics of effective communication and listening, critical and creative thinking, and an emphasis on personal responsibility and self-discipline.*

*Effective conflict resolution education programs can:*

*Enable children to respond nonviolently to conflict by using the conflict resolution problem-solving processes of negotiation, mediation, and consensus decision-making. Enable educators' ability to manage students' behavior without coercion by emphasizing personal responsibility and self-discipline. Mobilize community involvement in violence prevention through education programs and services, such as expanding the role of youth as effective citizens beyond the school into the community.*

*Four common strategies for approaching conflict resolution*

*Experts identify four school-based conflict resolution strategies that can be replicated in other settings. These are commonly referred to as:*

1. *Peer Mediation,*
2. *Process Curriculum,*
3. *Peaceable Classrooms, and*

4.  *Peaceable Schools.*

*In all four approaches, conflict resolution education is viewed as giving youth nonviolent tools to deal with daily conflicts that can lead to self-destructive and violent behaviors. It is up to each local school district to decide how conflict resolution education will be integrated into its overall educational environment. The expectation is that when youth learn to recognize and constructively address what takes place before conflict or differences lead to violence, the incidence and intensity of that situation will diminish.*

*The program examples provided below empower young people with the processes and skills of conflict resolution. However, youth need to know that conflict resolution does not take precedence over adult responsibility to provide the final word in a variety of circumstances or situations. Conflict resolution has a place in the home, school, and community, but it can only supplement, not supplant, adult authority.*

*Peer Mediation approach*

*Recognizing the importance of directly involving youth in conflict resolution, many schools and communities are using the Peer Mediation approach. Under this approach, specially trained student mediators work with their peers to resolve conflicts. Mediation programs reduce the use of traditional disciplinary actions such as suspension, detention, and expulsion; encourage effective problem solving; decrease the need for teacher involvement in student conflicts; and improve school climate.*

*An example of a Peer Mediation program is We Can Work It Out, developed by the National Institute for Citizenship Education in the Law and the National Crime Prevention Council. The program promotes mediation, negotiation, or other non-litigating methods as strategies to settle unresolved confrontations and fighting.*

*One Albuquerque elementary school principal reported, "We were having 100 to 150 fights every month on the playground before we started the New Mexico Center for Dispute Resolution's Mediation in the Schools Program. By the end of the school year, we were having maybe 10 (fights)." Other elementary schools using the same Peer Mediation approach to conflict resolution education reported that playground fighting had been reduced to such an extent that peer mediators found themselves out of a job.*

*Process Curriculum approach*

*Teachers who devote a specific time — a separate course, a distinct curriculum, or a daily lesson — to the principles, foundation abilities, and problem-solving processes of conflict resolution are implementing the Process Curriculum approach. The Program for Young Negotiators, based on the Harvard Negotiation Project, is representative of this approach. Participating students, teachers, and administrators are taught how to use principled negotiation to achieve goals and resolve disputes. This type of negotiation helps disputants envision scenarios and generate options for achieving results that satisfy both sides.*

*In a North Carolina middle school with more than 700 students, conflict resolution education was initiated. The school used the Peace Foundation's Fighting Fair curriculum and a combination of components from various conflict resolution projects. After a school year, in-school suspensions decreased from 52 to 30 incidents (a 42-percent decrease), and out-of-school suspensions decreased from 40 incidents to 1 (a 97-percent decrease).*

*Peaceable Classroom approach*

*The Peaceable Classroom approach integrates conflict resolution into the curriculum and daily management of the classroom. It uses the instructional methods of cooperative learning and "academic controversy." The Educators for Social Responsibility curriculum, Making Choices About Conflict, Security, and Peacemaking, is a peaceable classroom approach to conflict resolution. The program shows teachers how to integrate conflict resolution into the curriculum, classroom management, and discipline practices. It emphasizes opportunities to practice cooperation, appreciation of diversity, and caring and effective communication. Generally, peaceable classrooms are initiated on a teacher-by-teacher basis into the classroom setting and are the building blocks of the peaceable school.*

*Studies on the effectiveness of the Teaching Students To Be Peacemakers program, a Peaceable Classroom approach to conflict resolution, show that discipline problems requiring teacher management decreased by approximately 80 percent and referrals to the principal were reduced to zero.*

*Peaceable School approach*

*The Peaceable School approach incorporates the above three approaches. This approach seeks to create schools where conflict resolution has been adopted by every member of the school community, from the crossing guard to the classroom teacher. A peaceable school promotes a climate that challenges youth and adults to believe and act on the understanding that a diverse, nonviolent society is a realistic goal.*

*In creating the Peaceable School Program of the Illinois Institute for Dispute Resolution, students are empowered with conflict resolution skills and strategies to regulate and control their own behavior. Conflict resolution is infused into the way business is conducted at the school between students, between students and teachers and other personnel, between teachers and administrators, and between parents and teachers and administrators.*

*In an evaluation of the Resolving Conflict Creatively Program in four multiethnic school districts in New York City, teachers of the Peaceable School approach to conflict resolution reported a 71-percent decrease in physical violence in the classroom and observed 66 percent less name calling and fewer verbal insults. Other changes in student behavior reported by the teachers included greater acceptance of differences, increased awareness and articulation of feelings, and a spontaneous use of conflict resolution skills throughout the school day in a variety of academic and nonacademic settings.*

*The effective conflict resolution education programs highlighted above have helped to improve the climate in school, community and juvenile justice settings by reducing the number of disruptive and violent acts in these settings; by decreasing the number of chronic school absences due to a fear of violence; by reducing the number of disciplinary referrals and suspensions; by increasing academic instruction during the school day; and by increasing the self-esteem and self-respect, as well as the personal responsibility and self-discipline of the young people involved in these programs. Young people cannot be expected to promote and encourage the peaceful resolution of conflicts if they do not see conflict resolution principles and strategies being modeled by adults in all areas of their lives, such as in business, sports, entertainment, and personal relationships. Adults play a part in making the environment more peaceful by practicing nonviolent conflict resolution when minor or major disputes arise in their daily lives.*

*Information for this feature from the U.S. Department of Education.*

Alone and far from home: in the caresystem

*Alex Saddington*

*I was fourteen when I first came into care. I had been on the run for about three months. In my earlier school years I had many difficulties. I had to have special help because of a speech and hearing problem. I was in and out of hospital a lot at this time and so missed quite a few days at infant and primary school. In the 3rd year they moved me out of school because of my behaviour. I started to muck around in class. This was because home life was unbearable: there were always rows between my mother and stepfather. He would keep hitting me and my Mum till I couldn't take it any more.*

*When I was about 10, I was sent to my first special school, the first of six I was to attend in addition to two secondary schools. No-one really explained things to me and I was very bored there. I suffered a severe overdose of painting and drawing. That seemed about all we were given to do for the next two years. Because we had no interests to occupy our time, we ran wild. But instead of seeing that the school routine itself was actually making things worse, the staff put the blame on us. I got labelled 'maladjusted'. I was sent off to my first residential school (they are called EBD schools now for 'emotionally or behaviourally disturbed' children) .*

*I ended up at a school 200 miles away from my home. I was relieved to be away from my stepfather, but I hated it because it was so far away. I could go home only for main holidays and it was too far for any of the family to visit me. I could never go out alone, my incoming and outgoing letters were opened and read, phone calls were listened to and there was no freedom or privacy at all – it was like an open prison. No-one from outside ever came to visit me or ask how I was getting on.*

*Shunted around*

*I went on to a further two schools like this one. The worst thing of all was being shunted around. No sooner had I begun to settle than I was uprooted and moved. I don't know why. Each time I had to leave my friends and in the end I never made any friends because I knew I'd be moving in the near future. The loneliness made me feel that nobody cared: I was out of sight, out of mind.*

*When I was 14 they decided residential
school was not the answer. My problems
really stemmed from home, so the
Education Department was no longer
willing to see it purely as an education
problem and after four years sent me back
home for the Social Services Department
to have a go. I knew it wouldn't work out
at home and it didn't. The problems were
just as bad, if not worse, than when I left
because my family had grown apart from
me and I from them in the years I'd been
away.*

*I went on the run. My Mum put me in voluntary care. I agreed because I saw it as the only means of getting away from my stepfather. First I went to stay with foster parents, then I moved to a children's home. There was a rule that you were taken to school in a yellow mini-bus with 'Social Services' written in large letters on the side. Any young person in care knows how that makes you feel and how degrading it is. Then I was moved back to the foster parents and they decided the school was too far away for me to travel there every day. They put me in a special school for the physically disabled, even though there was nothing wrong with me.*

*Obviously it wasn't right, so they moved me to a special school for 'maladjusted' kids. It was a joke. All we did was muck around for a couple of hours and go home. There were no proper lessons. Finally they found another secondary school where I settled for the last year of my education. Very little was expected of me because I had missed out so much and because I was in care. Two weeks before I was due to take exams, the Social Services Department moved me 20 miles away from my school. Because of the upheaval and stress, I didn't take the exams. I left the school aged 16 without any qualifications at all.*

*Not giving up*

*But I was still determined to get a decent education. After leaving school, I was lucky enough to get a place in college to study 'O' levels. Halfway through the course, I decided with Social Services that I no longer wanted to be in care. So it was agreed that I leave care and I went to live with my grandparents. I was forced to give up college, though, as I couldn't get a grant or money from the Department. No-one told me that I could have applied for a grant from the Social Services (under Section 27 of the UK 1980 Child Care Act). I went back to college. This time it was an 'A' level course, which I am now halfway through. I hope to go to University and one day work in social work management or in politics. I am still coming to terms with all that has happened to me, but feeling more hopeful at last.*

*I believe that:*

- No-one should be moved around in care
  or at school more than once or twice at
  the most.
- Children should not suffer because of
  professional blunders – either by
  Education or Social Services Departments.
- No-one should be sent 200 miles away
  from home: they should be sent
  somewhere within reasonable travelling
  distance.
- Children should have somewhere in a
  children's home for studying in peace,
  and someone to take an interest in their
  work.
- What social workers demand and expect
  for their own children should be what
  they demand and expect for children in
  their care – they shouldn't say or think
  that it is no part of their job to provide for
  a child any better than its own parents
  could have done.

- The Education Department have got to allow for our problems: after all we didn't physically, sexually or emotionally abuse ourselves.

- All children should be given the opportunity of learning – even if they are 'different' – and should not be made to paint or draw all day.

- Social Services should be a good parent – and all good parents want their children to have success in education.

# CONCLUSION

I wrote this book to help fellow child and youth care workers, foster parents, caregivers/guardians  that is working with children in order to improve them for the better.

When you come into a centre the first time as a person the behaviour of the children and the labeling they receive from others is that they are naughty children, and when you are a new worker when you start hearing and witness these behaviours you start seeing the child as naught child without understanding the child's behaviour. With this book I hope to break that way of thinking and let those who wants to be a role model in the child's life first learn to understand the child and find more child friendly ways to approach and build positive relationship with the child.

I have added my personal stories and ways in how i dealt with situation good and bad to let you as a reader understand what it is to be a child and youth care worker. I hope my book can inspire all those who purchases it to be better role models in lives of children.